THE COMMUNICATIONS CHALLENGE

a practical guide to media neutral planning

edited by Julian Saunders

This book is sold subject to the condition that it shall not, by way of trade or otherwise, be lent, resold, hired out, converted to another format or otherwise circulated without the publisher's prior consent in any form of binding or cover other than that in which it is published.
The contents of this edition are believed to be correct at the time of printing.
The copyright of the many contributors is acknowledged.

The moral rights of the listed authors has been asserted

First published in Great Britain 2004 by The Account Planning Group

ISBN   1-904623-06-9

British Library Catalogue in Publishing Data:
A catalogue record for this book is available.

Printed and bound in the UK

Contents

Contents (continued)

What this book is about

Don Cowley

> ... concentrating on the how ...

Why does the marketing industry continue to debate the issue of media neutral planning when surely the arguments have been rehearsed many times by pundits from every corner of the marketing communications industry?

There is a simple explanation. Whilst there are many views on who should do it, who is competent to do it, and how they should be rewarded, almost no one has been prepared to discuss *how* it might be done. So here is a book that tries to address that need. Our purpose has been to discover what seems to be best practice in channel planning. The authors have contacted as a wide a variety of sources as is reasonably feasible to piece together a picture of the current state of knowledge and understanding. Perhaps not surprisingly no single discipline or organisation has emerged as providing a ready solution to the demands of media neutral planning. The reality is that serious marketing people need to touch a large number of bases and strands of thought if they are to get the kind of overview that will permit a significantly more effective use of their budgets.

This is both a book to read and a reference book. It has been put together under the auspices of The Account Planning Group because it is strategy planners in communication companies who most recognise the value of multichannel thinking. The chapters contain some fifty examples from major marketing and communications companies plus, of course, a good deal of commentary from people who understand the issues. These are not all famous or glamorous examples but all of them, we hope, may be useful models for somebody trying to find a more enlightened way of dealing with the task of media neutral planning.

We hope the book will be of practical value to everyone in the marketing community. In particular, we hope that brand marketing people, faced with the inevitable dilemma of allocating limited financial resources between a multiplicity of channels, will find something in the text or the examples that helps them make a better decision. We hope they also recognise that the communication planning process is best accomplished by people with a variety of skills and experience working in collaboration.

Introduction

Julian Saunders

The big change

We rarely now have those 'water-cooler conversations' when people across the country say 'did you see that programme on the box last night.' The 20 million-audience show is a thing of the past, unless England reaches the World Cup final. Those moments when we now stop and talk to each other tend to be prompted by big news like 9/11, the death of Diana or of the Queen Mother, rather than by the Morecambe and Wise Christmas Special. In any one year events like these are unpredictable and can be counted on the fingers of one hand.

In place of mass media we now have a deluge of media choice and the notion that almost anything has the potential to be a medium. Digital technology, which makes those media multiskilled, challenges our assumptions about how to use them in communications programmes. The stats are dramatic:

- There are over 230 BARB-reported UK commercial TV channels, up from about 50 a decade ago.

- Direct mail pieces reached the 5.2 million mark in 2002, up from 2.2 million a decade earlier, an increase of 136% in volume.

- There are about 250 commercial radio stations; the numbers have doubled in a decade.

- There are 140,000 posters panels, with the big growth coming from the 96-sheet super sites (+43% from ten years ago) and the small 6-sheets

(+140% from ten years ago).

- In 2003 BRAD reports a total of 3130 consumer magazines, compared with 2,100 in 1990.

- In cinema, the multiplex has triumphed; the number of screens increased by 80% between 1990 and 2000, with admissions up by 60% over the same period.

- We cannot count the number of websites today; a decade ago the web was just breaking out of academia to reach early adopters.

- The Newspaper Society reports that there are now 1300 regional and local papers

- The numbers of national daily and Sunday papers has remained static, but the pagination and numbers of sections have increased.

- Other things that capture our time and money are music albums, video games and CD-roms: the numbers of each released each year has significantly increased over the past decade.

Yet these 'conventional media' are just part of the story because there is a whole business culture that sees almost any property as a potential medium.

Here is a brief 'typical day'. At the breakfast table the back of my pack of Frosted Shreddies introduced me to a new fruit and fibre bar. At my nearest sports centre I see Lucozade energy drink advertised on posters as I queue for my ticket. The local lido is sponsored by Evian and the brand name is written in large letters on the bottom of the pool. At my daughter's school soft drinks are dispensed from a large cabinet with a particularly appealing image of a frosted can of Coke. I stand reading a poster about STDs in the urinal of my local pub. When I log on to AOL to look at my emails a screen pops up yet again suggesting I buy broadband. Each person will have a different experience. The overall impression is that more messages are being actively or passively processed in more media.[1] There is much more 'media clutter'.

One of the most important developments is that the multiple grocers increasingly see themselves as media owners. A big promotional display, a gondola end, eye-level stacking are proven to sell more. Brand owners have to pay for the privilege and, at the time of writing, the supermarkets are planning to go further and install screens in stores. Given the muscle and innovative spirit of Tesco and Sainsbury's these may be more successful than the dark screens still found in some garage forecourts, which were an earlier attempt to 'capture the eyeballs' of waiting customers.

For business people it can be both disconcerting and exciting. Certainly, it is tougher and more expensive to reach mass audiences but, on the other hand, there is much more scope for imagination and a challenge to the status quo. We have called this *The Communications Challenge*. Our ambition in this book is to equip the reader with knowledge, methods and ideas for taking advantage of these changes. By being 'media neutral' and considering all the potential points of influence in the lives of customers we believe it is possible to find fresh, efficient and effective ways to communicate.

Responses to the big change

Language and definitions
The communications industry has been searching for fresh language. After 'integration' in the nineties, we have 'media neutral planning', a term which has not attracted universal acceptance. This is partly because it is a leaden phrase and partly because it can be misleading and suggest that this is something that only media planning agencies do. It's not. As we shall see, media neutral planning can only be achieved through collaboration, because it is about communications planning in general and not just a development of media planning. Individual companies have developed their own language but media neutral planning has, however, started to emerge as a common term so it is worth briefly defining it. Its remit is ambitious and, much like a political party, represents a broad church, which makes it difficult to pin down.

What is meant by media is broad
When we talk about media now, we do not just mean 'conventional media' as in TV, posters, press and radio. Media means all the means of contact, interaction, and influence in the lives of customers.

It is about upstream thinking and implementation
Media neutral planning can start at the fundamentals: what is our business idea? What is our sustainable difference? What is our vision and mission? What are we promising our customers? Media neutral planning can cover a broad spread of issues; the upstream and the downstream, the strategy and the implementation.

More specifically it is concerned with:

- Generating ideas (which are not necessarily linked to a specific communications solution) that solve business problems and help realise ambitions.

- Behaving like an architect: building a picture of how a brand should behave, communicate and sell with its own people, stakeholders and customers.

- Coherent messaging, because ideas that are not efficiently and well executed have little value.

Structures and relationships

How the industry will structure itself to deliver these ambitious definitions of role is not our main concern here, though this will be played out in interesting ways in the future. One consequence, which we are already seeing, is the setting up of new businesses, separate business units and co-ventures. There is a lot at stake for agencies, which is best understood by examining the motivations of the interested parties.

The client motivation

Clients want the best possible advice; advice which they can also believe in. They want to think that it is unbiased and disinterested advice. Each of us is the product of nature, nurture and experience, so we have inbuilt biases. Bias is unavoidable. But communications businesses are not, in general, set up to offer disinterested advice, because complexity in the media and brand landscape has spawned specialisation. Specialists tend, quite naturally, to favour their specialism in recommendations. It is also tough to be a generalist nowadays because there is so much to keep up with. Teams of specialists are therefore needed, but they are often located in different agencies. The different agencies have an interest in managing and executing projects in their chosen specialism(s). Of course, the advice that clients receive may be excellent and deliver results but the nagging doubt remains: is it disinterested and as unbiased as possible?

The agency motivation

People in agencies aspire to be respected and trusted as 'business partners'. The alternative, being described as 'suppliers', pains them. Some react by saying 'we are first class at what we do and will be respected for it', but for most that's unsatisfying. The market for client respect is also getting crowded. Ten years ago the ad agencies still held pole position, now there are several aspirants. Media agencies, in particular, are well placed with their broad-based view of the media options and more commercial cultures. From the evidence of this book media agencies are also investing heavily in research, which is bound to affect the future balance of power. They are also the most enthusiastic champions of media neutral planning, although they would be unwise to attempt to annex it. It will be interesting to follow the trade press in the coming decade.

The contents of the book

The principles of communications planning

Successful communications can be simply described as saying the right things to the right people in the right places at the right time (which also gets the result you wanted). The basic knowledge needed to do communications planning is an understanding of *how people choose and buy* in a given market.

So far, so simple. Here is the current and future challenge: the explosion in media choice combined with dramatic changes in the take-up of and use of technology means that our understanding of how people choose and buy may need to be revised or even radically rethought. The rate of change differs according to the mentality of the customers and the nature of the market in question, but the overall trend is clear.

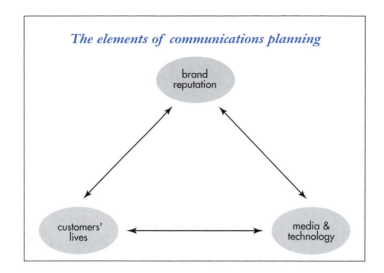

The elements of communications planning

brand reputation

customers' lives

media & technology

Of course, media and technology are not the only dynamics of change in communications planning. There are others – demography and shifting attitudes to brands, for example. Demographic change, as Keynes once said, is one of the most powerful forces in altering our culture. The role of women, work patterns, divorce rates, longevity and immigration make for a fascinating, ever changing and complex 'salad bowl' society. Similarly, attitudes to brands are constantly shifting. As a society we are generally more savvy and sceptical. People can decode the motivations behind campaigns. Communications planning is about the trinity of customers' lives, brand reputation and media/technology. The ambition of much of the content of this book is to show how thinking about the three corners of communication planning are brought together by new ways of thinking, working and generating ideas.

Much has been written elsewhere on demography and brands.[2] Our main theme is media and technology because it is where we observe the big structural changes. Here, in summary, is what we might call 'the thinking response', which describes the content of this book.

New models of understanding are being developed and older models are being evolved.

Research methods have been developed and substantial investments in proprietary research made.

Working processes have been developed that embrace multidisciplinary teams in the generation of and execution of ideas.

The need for ideas is greater than ever – to inspire organisational change as well as act as the glue for communications.

Effectiveness analysis is also presented with complications that have to be grappled with to justify investment.

The chapters and their contents

The structure is sequential but each chapter links to and overlaps with the next, rather like a jigsaw puzzle. The content is organised as follows:

Chapter 1 The important changes in media and technology and their consequences.

Chapter 2 The kinds of knowledge and customer insights that are now needed.

Chapter 3 How creative ideas galvanise campaigns and how to organise a team.

Chapter 4 How media channels may be selected and combined for maximum effect.

Chapter 5 How evaluation methods have to change to embrace the multichannel world.

1. The Planning Context

We provide more detail on the macro changes in media and technology and identify eight consequences and implications: media fragmentation, multi tasking, the value of the big idea, the liberation of new models of brand building, the potential for backlash, regulation and reputation, the power of editor brands and the growth of cross platform media deals. We identify some trends for the near future and finally, we put media neutral planning in the broader context and answer the question-how important is it in marketing today?

2. Knowledge into Insight

Ten years ago brand health could be analysed through the relationship between customers and brands. Now it's a three-cornered study that includes media. The chapter reviews how older models of brand analysis and segmentation have been evolved to include the media relationships. New methods of segmentation have been introduced that take media as the starting point not an afterthought. Of particular interest is the work of Diageo and Unilever, which is summarised here. Both companies have devoted energy to revising their processes and the way they train their people.

The growing volume of customer data that companies hold have stimulated the data analysis business to mine it for useful insights. Observational research has grown because, in the end, no amount of segmentation or data analysis quite captures real life nor can it do justice to the complex and protean way media are used, especially amongst the young. We show how 'where, when and how' a customer is available is as important as what that person thinks about a brand. It provides the platform for effective channel planning, which is the theme of Chapter Four, and needs to built into research from the word go.

In many organisations the word 'insight' is now used instead of 'research' and job titles have changed to reflect this. This is a response to increased complexity and volumes of research and data. Research is an activity that has to lead to the benefit of 'insights' or of making things as simple as they can possibly be in order to be useful. So this chapter concludes with a menu of collaborative methods, or 'workshops', designed to bring a multidisciplinary team together so that knowledge can be sifted for insights. Insights into brands, competitors, customers, and ways of communicating are the vital mental stimulus needed for creative work, which is our next chapter.

3. Creative Inspiration

Media has been defined as all the points of contact, influences and 'moments of truth' in the lives of customers, so doing the creative work becomes much more challenging and important. At minimum, creative work needs to provide the 'glue' that holds together a multimedia campaign, no mean task as different media have to carry different messages to different audiences and play specific roles within an overall plan. We examine different strategies for making coherent promises and illustrate them with mini case histories. What is the creative glue that holds it all together and what challenges does it present for creative people? We start with the simple models of 'identity only'; we look at the enduring appeal of advertising symbols, brand icons and creative theme integration.

The ambition for the truly 'big idea' is to influence or even radically change the whole organisation, to act as a focus and a rallying call to the people who deliver service and products as well as those who produce communications.

The chapter also has insights from creative directors into 'how to think neutral' and practical tips on how to set up the team to deliver a campaign. A development process and planning tools are provided which improve the chances of having a big idea, which can then be executed and evaluated with conviction by a multidisciplinary team.

4. Channel Planning

Channel planning is about building a picture of all the media and messages and how they fit together to meet the objectives of the brand. It is like being an architect; the channel planner needs to be both artist and scientist. All the different elements need to perform in a complementary way to meet individual objectives and to add up to an impact which is greater than the sum of the parts.

The bedrock of channel planning is understanding the tools of the trade. The chapter starts by looking at the latest thinking on how to classify and understand the qualities of individual media, which are also changing with the impact of digital technology. Direct response, for example, can encompass many different media, each of which has its own distinctive qualities. The internet presents a fresh classification challenge because it is really many different media that can deliver a broad range of outcomes from rational knowledge/response to emotional/brand building.

Individual media remain resolutely separate in their measurements methods. An important area of innovation is therefore the creation of a 'common currency' so that media can be compared on the same basis. We look at three approaches: scoring channels/media against their ability to achieve certain tasks; assessing them by 'customer contacts'; and a large-scale survey of leading media brands which maps them by image, positioning and personality.

The chapter concludes with 'optimisation' -how hard data, soft data and judgement can be combined in a process to refine a plan. We also show how a collaborative decision making process and judgement are valuable in delivering insight and helping to make a plan more distinctive.

5. Evaluation

The final chapter could equally be where we start the book. Communications planning involves understanding complex variables. As much simplicity as possible is required at the start to define the desired outcome of any activity. A straightforward evaluation matrix is provided to help achieve this simplicity. Evaluation needs to be as simple as possible and no simpler; there are, however, some complexities that have to be wrestled to the ground:

- Most plans use multiple channels and media.

- Channels/media perform different tasks within the plan.

- There is a multiplier effect from using channels in combination.

Evaluation needs to untangle these variables – to what extent have individual channels achieved their objectives within the overall mission and what is the cumulative or combined effect? There are barriers to success:

- Evaluation methods tend to be aligned with channels they were built around.

- Response-oriented media (DM and web) tend to emphasise short-term effects and immediate measurability whilst other media have tended to concentrate on long-term effects and brand equity.

- To make things more complex still, technology (especially digital) is making individual media multiskilled.

The chapter provides up-to-date advice on different evaluation techniques to assess a brand's 'momentum' with public relations, direct marketing and online. It also shows practical examples of how to disaggregate the effects of individual activities from the whole picture. It assesses the appropriateness of using econometrics and statistical modelling. It concludes with a brief survey of some of the latest purpose built and single source approaches, which have received significant investment from media agencies.

Evaluation can sometimes be off-putting or 'too difficult.' Amongst other things we do not know how the human brain works. Robert Heath put it this way: *'most brand information tends not to be actively sought as passively acquired ... yet most research is based on rational Cartesian measures and these are very poor at eliciting the factors and motivations that underlie intuitive behaviour.'* [1] A purist will always be able to identify a weakness in an evaluation method, but it is still better to be approximately right rather than absolutely wrong.

Successful evaluation is clear about how the particular brand in question is built and the outcomes it seeks from communications and it designs in methods at the beginning and not at the end.

Case histories and examples

We have included as many practical examples as possible. A separate case history index is provided. If there is one thing they have in common it is this; only powerful promises break through. *'Promise, great promise is the soul of an advertisement'* said by Dr Johnston, can be adapted for today. In world of media overload, great choice and savvy customers, a brand needs to make a potent promise, have a visceral understanding of its customers, behave distinctively in the marketplace and then keep its promises in everything it does. For successful growth brands this is the recipe that makes for 'sustainable differentiation', and the flavours are stronger these days.

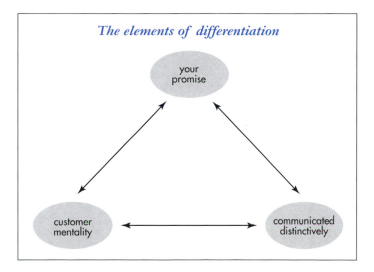

The importance of collaboration

Communications planning requires more science to gain knowledge and design evaluation. More art is needed to uncover insights, to build a picture of how communications can work and to provide the creative inspiration that holds it all together. The balance has to be just right. Too much science and it becomes arid. Too much art and self-indulgence creeps in. How do you get the balance right? Nothing beats teamwork between people with different skills and enjoyment of the whole messy reality of how campaigns are born. That's why we have included the section in Chapter Two on collaborative methods. If you get the right people together, it can be the best part of the process.

The preconditions for successful media neutral planning

There are significant barriers to doing media neutral planning successfully. The contributors to this book have found that it is best to flush them out at the start, because the set-up is vital and can determine success or failure. Here are three big barriers that are worth addressing head on.

1. Client budgeting

It is generally accepted that customers form their impressions of a brand or company holistically. Jeremy Bullmore puts it eloquently: 'we build an image as birds build nests, from the scraps and straws that we chance upon.' [3] But companies do not, in general, budget their customer communications holistically. Customer services, public relations, database management, and advertising often sit in separate financial pots, controlled by different people.

Some car companies, like Mercedes, have addressed the issue radically by taking control of the dealer network, because reputation depends heavily on consistency between the car itself and the experience at the dealer. Others, like Ford, have worked hard to achieve 'alignment' in the way the brand is experienced. Centrica have reorganised around customers rather than products and if they realise their vision theirs will be an influential case history.

2. Noticing only the things we understand

How we study the influences that affect customers (as they choose and buy) can have an impact on all that follows. It is what we might call 'the starter question' that sets expectations. Start in the wrong place and you can end up in the wrong place. For example, if the sources of influence investigated are just a list of preselected paid for media – TV, press, posters, DM, radio – then the solution proposed is likely to be some combination of these. It might be fine, but it might also miss something more fundamental. Communications planners need to develop 'the art of looking sideways'.[4] What are the stories and myths about the brand? What are its associations and what do its users look like? Is the brand or the category colour coded in some way? Do certain brand archetypes dominate, if so, why and what does it mean for the types of communication used? This inevitably means engaging people in the process who see the world differently, because none of us has a completely neutral mind (or 'tabula rasa') as we address the communications challenge.

3. Human nature

The best team is likely to be one with plenty of biases and expertise, combined with the ability to collaborate and listen. But listening is hard work and, if we are honest, not that common a skill. As soon as we start to absorb information on a project, we organise it in our minds, develop hypotheses and, often, we stop listening. So there is still one vital ingredient to successful media neutral planning – goodwill and a preparedness to park our prejudices and interests at the door for the greater good and the greater profit of the client.

Summary

For media neutral planning to progress it will need to be championed by hard-headed pragmatists and open-minded optimists. The former are needed to confront the barriers to success and clear them away as much as possible, while the latter have to inject a vital spirit of openness and cooperation. This book is our contribution. We think it is realistic, optimistic and above all packed with examples from which to learn.

By identifying and commenting on best practice in the marketing industry we hope this book will serve as a 'how to' manual for the practitioner: how to find insights, how to open up the options, how to put combinations together, how to make it all coherent. And, last but not least, how to measure that this is time and money well spent.

Notes and References

(1) Robert Heath *The Hidden Power of Advertising, Admap* Monograph #7 (WARC, Henley-on-Thames 2002)

(2) Wilmott and Nelson *Complicated lives* (Wiley 2003) – a succinct and useful account of how British culture is changing, with implications for business.

(3) Jeremy Bullmore *Behind the Scenes in Advertising* (Admap publications 1998)

(4) Alan Fletcher *The Art of Looking Sideways* – a primer in visual intelligence (Phaidon)

Chapter One

The Planning Context

Julian Saunders

The push-pull effect

The big change in media and technology is a combination of push and pull. As we have seen, there is much more supply. The arrival of a new medium causes commentators to predict the demise of older media; it was thought that TV would kill the press and that the web would have a similar effect on direct mail. The evidence of media expenditure is that there is more money spent on more media *(see below)*. So each new medium adds to the list of options for marketers to consider.

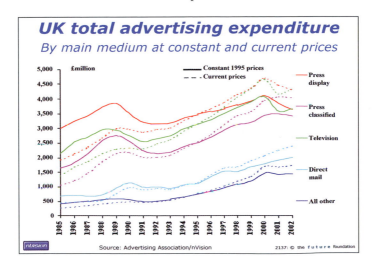

UK total advertising expenditure
By main medium at constant and current prices

Source: Advertising Association/nVision   2137: © the future foundation

Oversupply leads to ultra-competitiveness as media brands battle for audience and readers. Media seek out the fresh, the surprising and the new, expose it to our gaze, then overexpose it and continue seeking out the fresh, the surprising and the new. The media, therefore, act as a cultural force for education and stimulating change, especially in trying out new technology.

The take-up of technology

At the same time there is generally a rapid take-up of new technology. Certain categories are undergoing big changes as technology increasingly allows marketers to leap over previously insurmountable barriers. For example the Tesco Clubcard scheme, which has some 13 million members, is capable of routinely mailing the membership via a system which is capable of generating thousands and thousands of mailpack variations.

The topline numbers and projections show fundamental change is happening in the digital and database arena:

- 24 million adults, or about 50% of the 15+ population, used the internet in the last six months. It is expected to increase to 56% of the population by 2007. Nearly all internet service providers are now concentrating on upgrading customers to broadband.

- There are around 35 million mobile phone subscriptions. As the market matures in terms of penetration the focus has turned to upgrading and the enhanced functionality of 3G.

- Digital TV penetration is 40% in 2003 and is expected to reach 80% by 2012.

- In a DMIS survey, 61% of companies believed that the mail would increase in importance in the next five years. This reflects continuing investment in databases, which are enabled by digital technology.

Source: The Future Foundation, nVision survey, Direct Mail Information Service

It is as if the dotcom boom was simply a revolution ahead of its time. In the immediate aftermath of the dotcom bubble bursting, it was businesses that grasped the benefits of digital technology. Most people who work in an office have experienced the difference and have taken what they have learnt into their personal lives. At home, on TV, broadcasters actively promote other means of access; via websites, texting or the remote control. Arguably, the BBC leads the pack in helping to turn Britain into a society of multichannellers.

The multiskilling of media
The web and digital technology also undermine the conventional wisdom of what individual media do best. The web, for example, which is really several media inside one wrapper, can be used to promote awareness, generate response, provide

customer service, information and fulfilment. Direct marketing has grown as brand owners have invested in databases and analysis. Take a fortnight's holiday and your doorstep will illustrate it – there will be plenty of mailings from financial services companies looking to win a new customer, but there will also be a couple of customer magazines and an invitation to a preview from companies who are prepared to invest in keeping their best customers. Much of the growth in direct mail comes from companies using it in a non-traditional way.

Customer power

Digital technology empowers customers. In many markets, especially high ticket or high interest markets, it is used as a research tool as well as a channel for buying. First Direct, the pioneer of telephone banking, now reports that over 50% of its transactions are online. First Direct is also in the vanguard of developing text messaging as part of their service. NOP research shows that 28% of people who buy in shops have researched their purchase online beforehand. The early users of broadband simply do more of everything online than those with dial up connections. Broadband at home penetration in 2003 is 7% and is expected to rise to 19% by 2007. However, as 28% of adults say that they are very or quite likely to get the technology in the next six months (2003 data), this seems conservative, especially as nearly all internet service providers are cutting prices and promoting heavily.

Here are some of implications and consequences of 'the push-pull effect'.

Media fragmentation and the decline of the water cooler moment
The morning after one of those 20 million-plus TV ratings shows, like 'the death of JR', saw many water cooler encounters. 'Did you see?' conversations fed off common experiences. These are increasingly rare. There are 'A list celebs' to talk about, but not many. The pages of *OK! Magazine*, *Heat* and *Hello* are mostly filled with B, C and D list celebs and minor royals. Quite apart from the cultural effects, it used to be much easier to reach broad audiences, especially on television.

From the evidence of the IPA Effectiveness Awards, the most effective campaigns increasingly use three or four channels. There is more investment in media research to arrive at plans that marketers can be confident will reach their customers. Trade associations (like the Radio Advertising Bureau, the Direct Mail Information Service and The Interactive Advertising Bureau) have been beefed up to advance the case for their medium, investing in research to prove the case. It means that planners are equipped with better and deeper knowledge of individual media.

Multitasking and clutter
The media explosion vies for our time, but there are still only twenty-four hours in the day. The result, increasingly, is simultaneous use of media. One American study[1] showed that 50% of the time adults are engaged in simultaneous media use like phoning whilst watching the television, texting whilst listening to the radio, in fact doing almost anything whilst listening to the radio. Media can switch from background to foreground and back again in seconds, especially amongst the young

as we see in the study by Everyday Lives in Chapter Two. As more and more media, such as mobile phones, PDAs and broadband are 'always on', multitasking becomes a state of mind.

The implication is that bespoke research is increasingly needed. Industry research can be offputting; it shows fragmenting audiences that may be increasingly expensive and/or difficult to reach. The solution is to build a more intimate picture of the customer. What is his/her media world? How does he/she multitask with media and what are the individual influences of media? How are media used to choose and buy in the category? When is the brand important to the customer? What are 'the moments of truth' or 'connection'? Is there a more distinctive way of getting close to the customer? Out of this knowledge can come more effective, efficient and distinctive plans.

Media clutter can also influence how campaigns are budgeted. Instead of setting budgets and objectives first and then planning a campaign, a task-based approach can be helpful. It may be worth also asking the question: given our audience, objectives and level of marketplace clutter, what budget do we need? Looking across Europe, TV clutter levels are dramatically different, which might cause a pan-European advertiser to consider investing more for a better return in certain markets and reducing expenditure elsewhere.[2]

Fragmentation as a stimulus to the search for the big idea

Unless you are prepared to become 'a celeb', buy 'A list' endorsement or get reported on the television and the front pages, it is tougher to reach mass audiences. Few people other than Richard Branson have the appetite or the money for it. The consequence is that the big idea becomes a Holy Grail. A big idea is something that escapes its boundaries, becomes popular or even famous and therefore delivers value way beyond the media expenditure. Sometimes it is an ad, or an event, or it can be an eye-catching promotion that is so surprising and attractive that everyone is talking about it. Media fragmentation is one of the prime reasons why clients increasingly want, and agencies strive for, popular or even famous ideas rather just an ad or a promotion. The majority of campaigns do not reach these dizzy heights. The ambition for most is to provide coherence to a diverse set of communications – an organising idea – which is challenging enough.

Liberating other models of brand building

The conventions of brand-building as invented by the packaged goods brands of the 1960s are alive and well and with us still. 'Awareness' and 'reputation' are created on television, and sales are stimulated at point of sale through good display and an offer (plus variations on this basic theme). In software speak, it is still the 'default option' for many brands.

However, the rise and rise of digital technology and the media explosion, means new and different ways of connecting with customers:

- *Customisation* – digital media allow you to tailor the offer and for customers to talk back. In this model advertising, PR and direct marketing are used as gateways to the main relationship-building medium, which is online, where customers spend time configuring the brand or offer for their needs. Airline ticketing is the classic example.

- *Combinations* – different media are used in different ways to connect with customers. The brand tracks its customers through their everyday lives creating a multiplier effect by connecting with them at critical moments.

- *Sacrifice and overcommitment* – a particular favourite of challenger brands.[3] A brand chooses to be the most dominant and creative user of a particular medium in its category; a way of breaking through fragmentation by concentrating investment and energy.

- *Experiences* – creating events or experiences that bring customers into close contact with the brand, achieving awareness, knowledge, data capture and even sales through a single experiential campaign. Because media mediate between a customer and a company, this can trigger a counter trend. A truly personal letter, personal contact and, to use the jargon, 'face time' can be a way to break through clutter and make a connection. It is an expensive way to market but, assuming that you are able to identify the most valuable customers, it may be cost effective.

- *Retail environments* – once there were thousands of retailers and one major TV channel, and now there are hundred of TV channels, thousands of other media and only four major grocery retailers. So, the store has become a place where brand owners can be confident of an encounter with their customers.[4] It makes instore more than just a place for promotion; it becomes a brand-building event. Increasingly, this leads to partnerships between brand owners and retailers to build brands and categories. Merchandising and point of purchase are areas for innovation; for example, using the senses – sight, sound, touch, smell – to entice, intrigue and promote. In a sense, this model starts at the other end from the 1960s model above and works backwards into general advertising.

And, of course, other exciting and novel variations on the above are possible. At the heart of these developments is the search for heightened involvement with customers which improves the chances of affecting behaviour and engendering loyalty.

Be careful of backlash

Customers have become more knowing about the media and marketing game. The TV series *Pop Idol* invites millions to talent-spot and participate in the packaging and launching of 'a product'. Everyone is a marketer now, and a fair proportion of the population has been to a group discussion. People have become good at seeing the strings being pulled on the marionette.

At the pressure-group end of the spectrum we have Naomi Klein and George Monbiot, who see commerce invading our lives, politics and landscapes; the media is portrayed as a form of pollution. These ideas leak into the mainstream – *No Logo* and *Captive State* have been on the bestseller lists – and reawaken the shade of Vance Packard. The adman of old, once 'a hidden persuader', can become an unwelcome intruder from the self-interested world of commerce.

But you do not have to be politically motivated to get irritated by a message popping up as you try to send an email. Customers have become stroppier for a mixture of reasons – they know the branding game, they are short of time and they know what good service is nowadays. So media and technology may create more opportunities for heightened involvement, but for some people, it is just irritating.

The implication for marketers is the need for greater sensitivity about how messages and campaigns are being received or even used. A brief visit to adbuster.org will illustrate what can happen when a brand becomes the object of derision. Or just watch a group discussion of teenage boys deconstructing an ad – it can be bracing. Avoid sending a customer to the website only to frustrate them with graphics and a ten-minute download time; they may not yet have broadband. How people choose to use and react to communications can undermine reputations.

Regulation and reputation

The range of media available to agencies and advertisers is also a temptation. Agencies have always pushed at the boundaries of the acceptable to gain profile for themselves and advantage for their clients. But they have been saved from their worst instincts by a paternalistic regulatory regime.

For 'conventional media' the rules of engagement are well known. TV and radio are pre-approved for airing. The ASA has published detailed codes of practice and raps the knuckles of miscreants. The result is that advertising rarely commits a grave offence against factual inaccuracy or public decency. A poster for Wonderbra carrying the line 'Hello Boys' may have caused a frisson of disgust in some quarters, but it was, in truth, tame stuff. Peruse a lad's mag or flick through post-pub TV channels, and advertising seems very restrained by comparison. The banning of tobacco advertising is also a blessing in disguise for the communications industry because it removes a stinking fish from around the neck. It was not good for the industry's standing to be promoting the indefensible.

However the industry can still attract opprobrium: the areas of advertising to children, the use of databases and the web are risky for corporate reputation. Pester power was not really created by advertising. The deeper causes are an interaction of demography, economic confidence and the media which have produced the modern 'democratic family' with all its complex negotiations between mum and the kids, mum and dad, mum and the new partner, dad and the kids, the new partner and the kids and so on. But this defence will not necessarily stand because advertising is highly visible and parts of the political nation need scapegoats in order to promote tougher regulation. In the arenas of 'data' and 'digital' regulation is evolving. For the practitioner it is worth registering an interest with the DMA and the Interactive Advertising Bureau who make it their business to be up to date and to lobby for fair regulation. If European data protection regulation comes into force direct marketers will be required to ask people to opt in; perhaps it is wise to prepare now for such an eventuality. A healthy slice of common sense and self-restraint are also needed in order to pre-empt something more draconian. Parts of the web still feel like the wild west; a place of libellous gossip, devastating viruses and porn. If you choose to provoke, for example, a viral marketing campaign, you have to be prepared for your name, brand and holding company to pop up in the most surprising places, anywhere in the world. The ubiquity of the mobile phone also presents an exciting new way to promote but this needs to be balanced against the fact that it is above all a private medium and one, therefore, where opting in matters even more.

Editor brands

With the Niagara of choice comes selection and the importance of 'editors', brands that we entrust our time to because they share our tastes. Often these are more than editors; they are a part of our identities. They pass the 'I am a …' test as in 'I am a *Guardian* reader, a *Sun* reader, a *Radio 4* listener' and so on. They succeed in spite of, and perhaps because of, the increasing volumes of media to consume.

The web is a prime territory for the growth of new intermediaries which actively seek information or edit on our behalf. An individual may have several online intermediaries –professional (like Brand Republic or The Marketing Society), personal (Amazon), or travel (Opodo). Sainsbury's and Tesco, which increasingly see themselves as media brands, are editing for their customers – everything from recipes to financial services. It's not that surprising when we consider how much of a customer's time, attention *and* expenditure the big supermarkets enjoy.

Cross-platform dealing and partnerships

With the dramatic increase in media supply come two consequences:

- Consolidation of ownership (a hot topic for the regulators).
- Cross-platform media brands.

The BBC is currently the most powerful example of a cross-platform media brand. Already strong in broadcast and publishing, it actively promotes its online presence. For advertisers this opens up a different kind of relationship with media owners, who can be seen as potential partners in cross-platform deals involving PR, sponsorship, promotions and advertising. A good example is Emap, in the final chapter of this book, who put together a multifaceted deal for Fosters lager.

For media brand owners, it is a way to escape from the commoditising effects of dealing on a cost per thousand basis and take a larger share of promotional budgets. The advertiser can both get closer to customers and stimulate sales. Many media brands are generally much more important in people's lives than other types of brand, so it makes sense for advertisers to see them as partners in connecting with their customers and not just as a channel for targeting them.

What next?

The future is unknowable but here are some predictions that appear to be safe:

Generational change will affect our culture and the way people use media. The teenagers we meet in Chapter Two, courtesy of Everyday Lives, will grow up and feel even more confident and empowered in their use of media than their predecessors. Many of them will have their own media – such as personal networks and websites – which opens up the rich territory of marketing to communities of peers. It will require sensitivity and fresh thinking for brands to be accepted as partners in this arena rather than be rejected as intruders. But marketers will seek to take advantage of the ultra-efficient nature of 'peer-to-peer marketing' in the knowledge that good word-of-mouth is one of the best possible forms of advertising there is. Few however will succeed in 'unleashing an idea virus', and some will try, only for it to backfire.

The volumes of customer data will grow. The promise of Customer Relationship Management will be pursued by more and more companies as a route to profit through retaining and developing their best customers. This will place a premium on three things:

- Customers opting in to receive commercial messages either because they want to or have been paid to do so.

- Ownership of useful data.

- Intelligent and imaginative analysis of data.

The essence of successful communication – delivering the right message to the right person at the right time – should, in theory, become ever more possible.

Digital technology will be used by more and more people. As penetration of internet access reaches the 'late majority' and 'the laggards' in the adoption curve, the emphasis is switching to increased usage and trading up to broadband. Here are some projections:

	2003	2007
% 15+ pop. using internet	50	56
% HH with digital tv	50	80
% HH broadband	7	19

Sources: Future Foundation, Interactive Advertising Bureau (NOP)

Broadband appears to enable the internet to fulfil its potential. It has all the characteristics of a technology that is undergoing a rapid adoption curve; 28% of the population say they are 'very likely' or 'quite likely' to get it in the next six months. Internet service providers are promoting broadband heavily with increasingly attractive offers.

The early data shows that users do much more online once they have broadband, which may be partly because they are typically early adopter 'media junkies' and 'information addicts'. But the data does suggest that the broadband world will be different from the dial-up world. More time is spent online and 'day part usage' peaks between 5pm and 8pm. This is likely to affect television viewing but may give a boost to radio as many like to listen whilst online. It is the range of different applications (see below) that take a leap forward amongst users that indicate rapid adoption is likely. If 3G mobiles are searching for 'the killer app' then broadband already appears to have several.

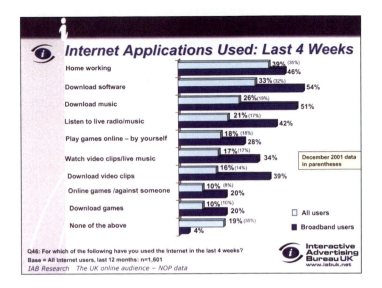

Internet Applications Used: Last 4 Weeks

	All users	Broadband users	December 2001 data in parentheses
Home working	39% (35%)	46%	
Download software	33% (32%)	54%	
Download music	26% (19%)	51%	
Listen to live radio/music	21% (17%)	42%	
Play games online – by yourself	18% (18%)	28%	
Watch video clips/live music	17% (17%)	34%	
Download video clips	16% (14%)	39%	
Online games /against someone	10% (8%)	20%	
Download games	10% (10%)	20%	
None of the above	19% (35%)	4%	

Q46: For which of the following have you used the Internet in the last 4 weeks?
Base = All Internet users, last 12 months: n=1,601
IAB Research   The UK online audience – NOP data

Interactive Advertising Bureau UK
www.iabuk.net

Television is already emerging as a gateway to a multimedia experience, the initial beneficiaries of which appear to be media brands. The BBC is the biggest educator in the use of multimedia, which would be positively Reithian of the corporation where it not for the fact that it is also cross-selling considerable interests in magazine and book publishing. People who are busy being entertained may not want to also go shopping online, but they may be happy to register an interest thereby delivering valuable 'propensity to purchase' data to media owners.

The things that give us pleasure – magazines, imaginative promotions, exclusive invitations, films, listening to the radio, soaps, vegging out in front of the television – will continue to give us pleasure. Novelty will continue to surprise and excite us. The generally high standards of TV ads will mean that people will be quite content to watch the ad breaks, in spite of new technology that enables them to be edited out.

New media opportunities will continue to be invented – remember 'on cow' advertising and 'crop circles.' Some will find a place in media plans, like advertising in public conveniences; others will fall by the wayside. Perhaps in five years' time we will find more TV screens, access to websites and 'polysensual experiences' when we do our weekly shop for groceries. For those who love to browse it may add to the experience. For time-pressured parents with a shopping list, it might be off-putting. For multiple grocers, it fulfils an ambition to select more things for their customers and to be 'media owners'.

The 30-second television commercial will be alive and well, as will all the other forms of so-called 'conventional media'.

There will be many more white vans on the streets delivering the fruits of online and catalogue shopping.

The wider context:
how important is media neutral planning to marketing?

The short answer is that it is increasingly important. Some historical perspective explains why. In the post-war period the four Ps of marketing – product, price, place and promotion – used to happen generally in that sequence. A product could be brought to market, promoted and be reasonably sure of demand because markets were growing and there were evident wants and needs to be satisfied.

Now marketers often start with the fourth P and ask: how can a brand be created or sustained with distinctive communication? They then work backwards into the capabilities of the organisation to ensure that promises can be kept. Successful growth brands today are 'culturally aligned'; external promise is aligned with internal culture and delivery. (This opens up another frontier and implies new kinds of partnerships between communications planners and experts in organisational change.)

There are several reasons for this: most markets are now mature and highly competitive; innovation mostly delivers marginal improvements rather than a great leap forward in performance and the obvious basic needs of consumer society have been satisfied. Differentiation therefore often derives from the way a brand is consistently communicated rather than because of any rational differences in performance. Demand has to be stimulated with distinctive and imaginative communication.

Fortunately (otherwise people in marketing and communications would all be out of work), societal and demographic change combined with increasing wealth in western economies constantly bring fresh needs to the surface, which are both psychological and practical. Here are some examples: wanting personal recognition or a sense of progress, expressing individualism or belonging; the desire for sensual pleasures, the quest for new experiences and the impulse to try new things; rising expectations of quality and service … and more. Uncovering these needs are often the 'insights' that provide the springboard for great ideas, innovation and plans.

Never has there been a better time to find distinctive ways to influence the way customers chose and buy. The proliferation of media and the take-up of technology generate an exciting palette of options for marketers. And some of the barriers to activity, such as increasing regulation, may even cause people to come up with better ideas.

Notes and References

(1) BIGresearch, March 2003 (sample size 7800)

(2) *'How to budget for healthier ROI' Admap*, Harper and Bridges issue 441, July August 2003

(3) Adam Morgan *Eating The Big Fish* (Wiley 2001)

(4) Andrew Harrison *'Let's innovate for chocolate'*, FT Creative Business June 2003

(5) Jan Rijkenberg *Concepting* (WARC 2001)

Chapter Two

Knowledge into Insight:

Market Segmentation and Beyond

Roderick White

> **Navigation box**
> Segmentation is fundamental
> The Diageo and Unilever approaches
> Media agency models
> The innovation and adoption approach
> Customer journey
> Data integration
> From knowledge to insight
> Insights, ideas and workshops
> Conclusion

Communication planning is a key element in marketing, and profound changes in the variety and structure of the available media channels drive the need to rethink our approach to it.

These changes make the success of marketing activity more than ever dependent on developing a profound understanding of who the target consumers are, how they relate to a category and the brands within it, and how they use media to gather information or form attitudes about the brands they buy.

So, it is no longer enough to know how many people are in the market for a product, or even what sort of people they are. Everyone can find that out. Marketers must somehow discover *why* consumers make the choices they do, and *how* these choices can be influenced, in the face of all the competitors an active market involves. This places a burden on marketing people to integrate their information sources, particularly by relating marketing data to media data. Inevitably this is an imperfect process, so it needs to be supplemented by the magic ingredient (now reflected in many client-side researchers' job titles): *insight*.

This chapter looks at two main aspects of getting and managing knowledge and insight about consumers – or people, as it seems more polite to call them. First, we look at some of the ways of identifying and defining the target audiences for marketing communications through different forms of segmentation; then we consider how new approaches are beginning to turn this knowledge about people into more useful, actionable insights to guide communication strategy, planning and execution. Finally, we look at the whole question of how to generate useful insights.

Segmentation is Fundamental

Customer segmentation has always been fundamental to marketing, but the increase in communication channel options has created an additional need to understand market segments through the media they respond to.

Early segmentations were demographic, based on age, sex, income group, etc. – data found in government censuses and readily obtained from survey respondents. The basic demographic breakdowns have become an established currency for all kinds of survey work. They have the great benefit that they can be used easily to compare different surveys and to relate, say, a brand survey to media audience research.

While this sort of segmentation is practical and useful – especially in relation to media planning, where it ties in with the buying currency of audience research – it is of course relatively crude.[1] Hence, much of the effort of the marketing industry has been directed towards improving and refining marketing segmentation information. Here are some of the main sources and techniques currently used:

- *Geodemographic:* starting with the Target Group Index(TGI)-based ACORN system, survey data on product and media usage has been combined with census data to create geodemographic classifications, which split the population into small neighbourhood clusters of similar-seeming people, reflecting the reality that we tend to be quite like our immediate neighbours. A range of geodemographic classifications is available from several suppliers.

- *Brand-based:* people are defined in relation to their usage of a given brand, and, more recently, their degree of commitment ('loyalty') to it. This is usually the starting point for applying additional forms of segmentation.

- *Media-based:* new thinking about media planning has led to a focus on how people relate to different media, and the development of segmentations based on media usage, attitudes to individual media and how and where people look for brand-related information.

- *Attitudes and values:* moving from what people are and what they do to what they think is a natural progression, though it has proved complicated to initiate. Apart from debates about what attitudes and values are – attitudes are more ephemeral, and may refer to almost anything researchers may wish to look into; values are more permanent, and reflect people's view of the world – there's the question of 'attitudes to what?' The category? The brand? Innovation? Shopping? Life, the universe and everything? Each *could* provide the basis for valuable insight.

- *Lifestyle and lifestage:* lifestyle relates to attitudes and values, but may be partly defined by social activity, key possessions, type and location of house (close to geodems), etc. Lifestage, especially useful in financial marketing, uses key transitions in life as focal points for understanding people's needs and priorities.

In practice, sources of knowledge about people that may be relevant to communications planning are many and various. The table below summarises some that are particularly useful.

Sources of consumer information

Personal Data:
- Address: electoral register, customer records.
- Purchase behaviour: direct users only – customer records.
- Contact record: call centre, complaints, web/email, etc.
- Preferences and interests: 'shopper' surveys, customer contacts.

Survey data:
- Behaviour and attitudes: ad hoc surveys – U&A, etc.
- Purchasing, media use: consumer panels.
- Media exposure and habits: media surveys, panels.
- Brand use and media habits: TGI, etc.
- Values surveys: RISC, Roper, etc.

Qualitative data:
- Observation/ethnographic.
- (Focus) groups.
- Depth interviews.
- Call centre, etc., staff reports.

While it is clear that personal data are the most valuable – especially for anyone with a direct marketing operation – there are obvious pitfalls. Even the most sophisticated databases will have knowledge gaps. Near-perfect knowledge about a customer – outside, perhaps, some B2B markets – is unattainable, which is a key reason why insight is needed to turn the data into useful material on which to act.

Examples of segmentation in action

A growing number of sophisticated models are beginning to appear in the market, from a variety of sources. Large advertisers have their own proprietary approaches; media planning agencies are increasingly active in this area, as channel choices have risen up the agenda; and market research agencies are also busy.

In general, these new approaches are described as 'multi-layered', 'holistic' or '360°'. They attempt to combine a variety of information about consumers, to provide an in-depth view of them. In particular, they aim to aid media neutral (and discipline neutral) planning by focusing on the relationships involved in the Customer-Brand-Media triangle.[2]

The Diageo and Unilever Approaches

Diageo

Diageo is the world's largest alcoholic drinks manufacturer. To ensure that company-wide learning is applied consistently, globally and to the best effect, it has developed a series of manuals called *The Diageo Way of Brand Building*. The core consumer-related element of this is called *Consumer Connection Planning*. The starting point for channel planning is the classification of consumers in the market for any brand into four groups based on their (ascending) level of brand commitment – *Availables, Acceptors, Adopters* and *Adorers*.

The second part of the planning process centres on using research and past findings to develop relevant insights into how barriers to conversion or heavier purchase (or other desirable behaviour) may be broken down in whichever of the four groups is judged to be the priority target, and using this understanding to select the appropriate marketing channels. In general, objectives that involve strengthening commitment to a brand point towards media advertising solutions while those that need the removal of barriers may require more promotional types of activity.

For a broader view of Diageo's process, see below.

How Diageo Does It

The core aim of Diageo's system is to select '…only those marketing disciplines that will most powerfully connect with consumers…[to drive] the measurable behaviour changes needed to deliver our consumer goals.' This requires an integrated plan for the brand which concentrates on selected activities, each with defined goals and designed to connect with the target consumers at a deep and motivating level.

The process revolves around analysing category consumers into groups – *(Rejectors), Availables, Acceptors, Adopters* and *Adorers* of the brand – as the basis for analysis, research, activity planning and subsequent evaluation. For each group, a consumer response model is developed, looking at responses to marketing activity at four stages; perception, consideration, the moment of choice and conversion. The analysis focuses on two key elements: things the company does to influence people; and things other people may do that influence target consumers.

This requires a clear understanding of factors that influence and/or discourage purchase by each group of consumers, and it has to be translated into specific activity goals that can achieve improved sales. Developing these goals is a five-step process – the 5 'I's: defining the *Issue*, gathering *Information*, developing *Insight* into what is required to achieve change, determining the specific *Implications* for action, and *Implementing* this action.

Action needs to be translated into specific marketing disciplines, and this depends on understanding how the target group responds to different channels, comparing appropriate disciplines and channels against past experience, and allocating budgets accordingly.

Source: Diageo

The example below shows how the Diageo targeting-by-specific-brand-commitment group can lead to a non-standard (for drinks) media choice.

Gordon's Gin – brand-building amongst high-value consumers

Diageo identified high-value gin drinkers (adorers & adopters) as a target for specific activity. A regular programme of witty letters from master distiller Hugh Williams targeted known high-value consumers. The mailing list was kept informed of developments such as new packaging. Ideas for fresh ways of serving gin when entertaining were also included. Crucially, coupons were used sparingly; this was a brand-building programme. Results were assessed by sales and brand measures but the 'shoals of thank-you letters' were also seen as a useful indicator.

Clearly the value of the DM & EDM (there was an online element in the programme) channels is that they could carry discrete campaign messages which might be irrelevant to less committed users.

Source: Craik Jones

Unilever

Unilever, as one of the world's largest packaged goods companies, has highly-developed systems for shaping marketing communication planning, embodied in a module called *Communication Channel Planning* (CCP) within the company's *Advanced Brand Communication* (ABC) process. CCP formalises the process of developing brand communication plans and budgets, using a suite of proprietary software as an aid.

The guiding principle is to put the consumer first, recognising that marketing works most effectively when all consumer 'meetings' (broadly, what direct marketers call 'touchpoints') with the brand can be integrated, and that by focusing on the consumer, channel neutrality can be successfully achieved.

The summary of the CCP module below serves to demonstrate that channel planning can only be effective when it is a natural extension of brand planning.

Unilever Practice

Channel selection starts once the outline programme of activities (defined in broad terms as, e.g. 'launch', 'build trial', 'active defence') has been defined for the brand, and a preliminary budget determined. Each activity is then taken through four steps:

- Define the target audience.
- Set measurable marketing objectives.
- Set measurable communication objectives.
- Evaluate and prioritise channels.

Target audiences are defined in at least one – preferably more – of three ways derived from a variety of research: volumetric, attitudinal and socio-demographic:

- *Volumetric* analysis identifies groups of consumers who are actually or potentially most valuable to the brand, in terms of sales, so targets may be defined in terms of loyal users, light users, etc.

- *Attitudinal* data provide a description of the attitudes, values and relationships with the brand that can inform creative strategies and provide a rounded picture of the sort of people that comprise the target audience.

- *Socio-demographic* data are described as rarely being useful for target-setting as such, but valuable for planning the use of traditional media, where they provide the buying currency.

As an example, the UK Surf target is defined as follows:

- Heavy detergent buyers, but at low price.
- Buy small packs of standard biological powders.
- Buy portfolio of brands: Surf + 3 others = 75% of purchases, (vs 32% for all households).
- Account for 70% of all Surf purchases.
- 3 distinct sub-groups; value; brand preference; habit.
- 25-54 C2DE part-time/non-working.
- Traditional outlook.
- Work just for money. Find saving difficult.
- Heavy TV viewers (soaps/game shows) and like ads.
- Read popular papers, women's weeklies.

Against this sort of target, marketing objectives are set which specify and quantify, e.g. increased penetration, or a higher share of requirements; and communication objectives, which are usually concerned with increasing awareness, knowledge of a key brand benefit, or specific brand values.

Finally, these objectives are used to evaluate candidate channels, rating each channel against a specific set of criteria:

- Budget parameters – what's the minimum threshold spend?

- Reach – how much of the target audience can we get to?

- Speed of effect – will this channel work fast enough?

- Communication quality – can this channel get our message across properly?

- Qualitative insights from the brand analysis – does the channel and its context fit with consumer expectations for the brand?

Based on this, all candidate channels are listed, then prioritised as the basis for detailed planning.

Source: Unilever

The system aims to ensure that full use is made of the Company's accumulated experience and knowledge, and of the wide range of research most Unilever brands have at their disposal. This is enabled, to a substantial extent, by tools available within the company's proprietary planning software.

Media Agency Models

Whilst Unilever and Diageo have brand-centred approaches to channel planning, media agencies have developed proprietary models in response to marketplace factors, principally media fragmentation, and the growing interest in media combinations and in media neutral and discipline neutral planning. Allied to these pressures is the fact that virtually all conventional media audience research is resolutely single-medium. In consequence, there is no common currency available to enable cross-media comparisons, multi-media schedule optimisation, etc.

As a result, media agencies have found it essential to develop their own ways of looking at consumers' relationships with the media as a whole, and – as far as possible – to tie this together with consumers' relationships with brands.

Mindshare: 3D
Mindshare has taken brand relationships as the foundation stone for its global proprietary study 3D. It combines the principles of Millward Brown's BrandZ study with social dynamics and media behaviour. MindShare believes that 3D delivers, in a single source, the most effective dynamics for effective strategic planning.

The brand relationships element of 3D parallels Diageo's 'brand commitment' approach. People are placed on one of five stages of a pyramid depending on the strength of their relationship with the brand. The levels range from a base level – Familiarity, where people have awareness and perhaps basic brand experience, through to Commitment, where the most loyal users are found and where they will use the brand over and above any alternative in the category.

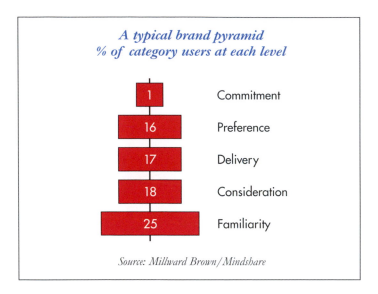

A typical brand pyramid
% of category users at each level

1	Commitment
16	Preference
17	Delivery
18	Consideration
25	Familiarity

Source: Millward Brown/Mindshare

3D demonstrates that different brands convert differently from one level to the next but, importantly, the Commitment and Preference levels account for a disproportionately high share of sales. Different targeting strategies are identified by differently-shaped pyramids.

Companies increasingly want to focus communications activities on heavy category users and high-profit customers. The 3D brand pyramids provide the basis for identifying the most potentially profitable target groups but 3D's strength comes from the inclusion of additional consumer information on relevant targets – who they are, what they own, what they think and how they behave – combined with in-depth information on their behaviour across an exhaustive range of communications channels.

As a result, MindShare has converted a proven, established brand equity model into a three-dimensional tool for strategic planning that incorporates channel selection. For a view of 3D at work, see opposite.

Example of 3D in action
– money talks and so does effective strategic planning

In this case study from Singapore, a change in targeting and channel selection increased advertising response to deliver more customers to the credit services of a major bank.

Bank customers switch accounts and other financial services very infrequently. The objectives set by this bank were particularly challenging: to significantly increase the number of new applicants for one of their credit services from outside the existing customer base – and to deliver within three months!

3D was applied to identify potential customers who were in a receptive frame of mind towards credit and who would therefore not need to be persuaded into the market. The emphasis could then be placed on communicating the brand's advantages rather than trying to attract people who were unfamiliar with the concept of debt or who had a negative attitude towards it.

3D identified a base of 223,000 customers of two major competitors who could be in the market for an alternative brand offer. Further 3D analyses explored the most appropriate communications channels to reach this fertile group.

The analyses suggested a radically different print schedule from that already used. For example, it eliminated the leading daily Singapore newspaper – a title which normally would never have been ignored but which is cluttered with competitive messages. It also recommended first-time use of both technology and finance print supplements and radio. 3D also demonstrated that the most lucrative target group was not adverse to direct communications and so a direct mail strategy was employed. All the advertising included a direct response mechanism.

The results exceeded all expectations. The bank had the highest pool of applicants for its credit service as a result of the new campaign strategy. All the selected channels produced a record number of direct response calls on the days when the advertising appeared.

Source: Mindshare

OMD: Communigraphics

Whereas Mindshare's model starts from brand reputation, this new model from OMD springs from a study of people's attitudes towards communications. It starts from the viewpoint that people participate in the media and communications not just as receivers but as processors and transmitters as well, and that conventional research misses a whole range of everyday transactions between consumer and brand. In consequence, the model uses a very broad definition of 'communications', including word-of-mouth.

Communigraphics clusters people into groups according to their attitudes to communicating and being communicated with. The attitude battery in the research includes aspects of personality, which provides a reasonably permanent and consistent view of a person's make-up (as opposed to attitudes to brands and media, which may be quite volatile and less deeply embedded).

As a result groups with similar demographic backgrounds can have very different communications profiles. For brief descriptions of two of these groups, see below.

OMD Communigraphics: two segments from UK pilot, 2001

Sociable Young Friends
- Active social life, revolving around a wide network of family, friends, lovers, colleagues from school, work, etc.
- Highly brand-oriented, avid followers of fashion.
- Love to talk, compulsive communicators; especially heavy texters.
- Like ads and enjoy talking about them with friends.
- Impulsive, novelty- & variety-seekers
- Full-time workers, income above average.

Free Spirits
- Well educated, good jobs, high incomes. High levels of job satisfaction.
- Thoughtful, make up their own minds about issues; prepared to have controversial points of view; don't need people to like them.
- Tend to have sharply defined, all-absorbing interests: technology, sport/fitness.
- Not great followers of fashion.
- Small social networks, revolving around work and clubs; little liking for parties or small talk.
- Hard to reach through advertising. Light TV viewers, heavy online users.

In the most recent version of Communigraphics, the survey data have been fused to the TGI database, thus providing access to all the brand usage and media behaviour of clusters, as well as the specific communications data collected in the Communigraphics survey. Thus detailed communications plans can be constructed to best reach particular clusters.

For example, segments with an extravert profile have larger networks and are more active processors of information, and are therefore valuable for a brand seeking to generate a groundswell of interest through word of mouth. By contrast, those with a more introverted profile often make it their business to read up about a subject or surf the web for information, while resisting the influence of advertising or sponsorship. Their value as influencers or brand advocates cannot be ignored because of their know-how, but PR, rather than advertising, is likely to be the best way to reach them effectively.

Carat

The Carat ALR (attitude, lifestage, resources) model recognises that effective channel planning needs to combine market segmentation with media attitudes. Given that different clients have different forms of segmentation, Carat has developed a way of operating that enables it to take client-generated market segments and then understand the values of the different media channels from the viewpoint of each segment.

The data bridge for this is an annual 'consumer connection survey' (CCS), which combines a U&A (usage and attitude) for the client's category with an extensive media consumption survey. The output can be expressed in a four-quadrant mapping which plots the values of the individual media for each segment of users.

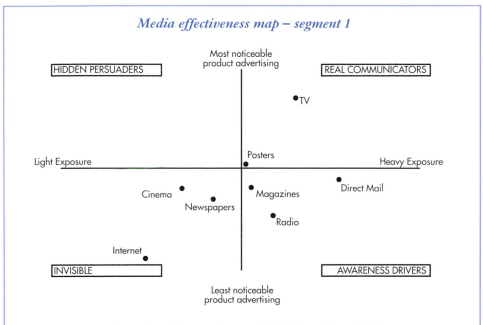

Media effectiveness map – segment 1

Source: Carat Consumer Connection Study (May to August 1999)
(see John Svendsen, Consumer segmentation and media, *Admap November 2000)*

This is a typical segment map. It illustrates how people in this segment tend to see TV as a 'real communicator' and the internet as an 'invisible' medium as it scores low on noticeability and exposure. Other user segments of the same brand may have very different 'maps', a finding which emphasises the idea that consumer segmentation is a fundamental part of effective media neutral planning.

The innovation and adoption approach: planning in evolving markets

Most people in marketing are familiar with the 'adoption curve', a segmentation that classifies potential customers by their willingness to embrace new ideas and purchasing behaviours. The idea has been borrowed from the academic world and it has proved to offer a robust way of dealing with the different marketing demands that arise as a product field develops from a new introduction to maturity. As the rate of innovation in markets speeds up, adoption models are increasingly relevant because they recognise that different targeting and communication channel strategies are needed at different stages in the development of a market or even a brand.

Typically, adoption segmentation identifies six customer groups who enter the market in sequence. They are normally called.

- Pioneers
- Early Adopters
- Early Majority
- Late Majority
- Traditionalists/laggards
- Ultra-traditionalists/laggards

The pioneers and early adopters are usually reckoned to make up some 15% of the customer potential in a particular market; the early and late majorities, or followers, are consistently responsible for about two thirds of the potential; with the traditionalists accounting for the remaining 20% or so. (That said, the example below shows higher proportions in the traditionalist group.)

The MicroMatch model

Interestingly, MicroMatch, a marketing consultancy that bases its approach on the adoption curve, identifies separate adoption groups for each market. So, for example, someone may well be an early adopter in motor cars but a traditionalist when it comes to shoes, a finding that seems to appeal to common sense. But this does imply that attempts to classify the whole population into adoption groups that will suit all markets are likely to be of dubious value.

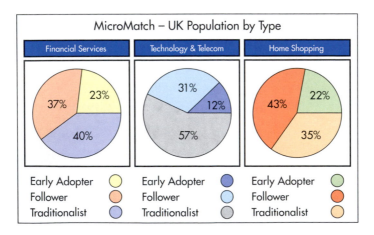

In cooperation with NOP & Equifax, MicroMatch Marketing has profiled the UK population by primary segments across a number of markets. MicroMatch identifies each adoption segment in research through its principal buying motivation. Ideas and conclusions about communications channel choice and the media choice given here are based on these buying motivations and are echoed to some degree in the MINI case history in Chapter Four.

Early adopters
The primary motivation of early adopters is self esteem, and early adopters need to feel that they are getting information before anyone else. Independent editorial and word-of-mouth endorsements are therefore important. 'Exclusive' offers using direct mail and advertisements in specialist media are likely to have particular appeal to early adopters.

Followers
Followers' primary motivation is affiliation – the desire to feel the approval of a larger consumer group. To attract followers quickly, investment in mass-market media and/or the widest spread of specialist media is required. Media coverage reinforces the fact that a product or service is in vogue. Positive brand associations become one of the bases of the competition to attract followers. Efficient well-organised PR programmes to support mass media advertising are important in achieving this.

Traditionalists
Marketing communications should give the customer a basic sense of security and reassurance, with the focus being on maintaining a positive perception of the brand. Brand presence has to be reinforced by mass media advertising aimed at developing instant recognition and familiarity, reinforced by consistency in product features and benefits and continuity of design and presentation.

Of course all communications 'rules' like these should be used within a consistent and cohesive marketing framework. PR is very often seen by marketers as an appropriate channel for brand launch activity, when early adopters are likely to be in the majority. Direct mail when combined with a customised early adopter, follower or traditionalist message will work at each stage of a market adoption curve. TV advertising can reassure followers that they are hot on the heels of early adopters, and with a different creative approach it can reinforce traditionalists' heartfelt need to stick with products and services they know and avoid risking a change.

Other research-based approaches
Two other types of segmentation deserve a brief mention, since they can significantly affect the way in which media and channel planning should be done.

The first comes from Malcolm Gladwell's much-quoted book *The Tipping Point*. The main argument in Gladwell's book is that new ideas are spread by quite small groups of people who happen to be especially well networked. If you can successfully find and reach the key communicators in a given market (and they may be different people in different categories and sectors), it is possible to accelerate the market presence of a brand very considerably.

The second has been around since the mid-1990s, when Geoff Bond and Steve Griggs identified the existence of *ad rejectors* – people who are considerably less responsive than the average to advertisements. This finding has since been refined by the observation that ad rejection varies according to medium, and the same people do not necessarily reject ads in all media, giving added strength to the now widely-accepted view that combinations of media are better than single-medium campaigns, always assuming the budget can stand it.[3]

Seeing media in the context of the purchasing process

If segmentation is the starting point for media neutral planning and the second stage is to understand people's relationship with the media channels, then the third analysis has to consider how the media channels are likely to affect the consumer as s/he travels through the purchasing decision process.

Mapping this process is not necessarily a straightforward task, because much of the behaviour may be unconscious and therefore difficult for research respondents to recall. Watching what people do (observation studies) may well be more valuable than interviews. The key task is to identify how each marketing stimulus fits into the consumer purchase process. Ideally, the end product of the analysis is a channel strategy built around consumer 'influence' points.

The customer journey

The idea of the customer journey is especially relevant to major and complex purchases, where the gestation of a decision may be quite long-term, and the range of touchpoints and, indeed, 'moments of truth' can be quite wide. The purchase of products like a car, a holiday, a pension plan goes through several distinct phases – see the diagram below which, though it may not work in quite such a tidy, logical way for everybody, provides a fertile basis for thinking about how best to contact people and influence their decisions.

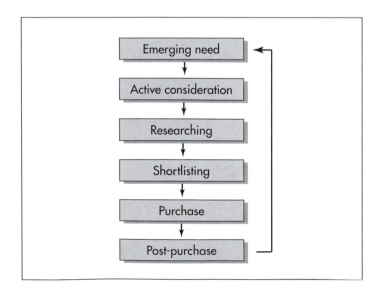

The dynamics vary by market, and different media will be relevant at different stages for each consumer, depending on whether the stage is active or passive. Similarly, journeys vary in length and complexity for different consumers. In financial services markets, this will depend, for example, on how savvy or interested the consumer is, as opposed to being less confident and less informed – which is why segmentation and the customer journey can be complementary.

Two examples show how customer journeys can inform contact strategies and activity. The first concerns a major durable purchase, a car.

The 11 stages in the car-buying journey – from purchase of current car

1. Post-purchase 'honeymoon'.
2. 'Non-interest' – reinforcing existing choice.
3. 'I need to replace this car some time in the not-too-near future.'
4. 'I/we are going to need a new car quite soon.'
5. Serious looking about.
6. Shortlisting.
7. Detailed investigation.
8. Shopping around.
9. Negotiation and payment.
10. Waiting for delivery.
11. Delivery.

The process starts literally as the consumer takes delivery of the latest car, and goes on in a continuous cycle. The first part (stages 1–4) of the process has two key characteristics: initially, the maker (or dealer) of the latest car is potentially in control' and the consumer is, as VW's agency pointed out in an IPA Award-winning paper, in an essentially passive mode. However, once the need for a new car emerges, the mode switches to active, and the consumer becomes far more open to the blandishments of other marques, models and marketing activities.

Each stage has its own specific features, and the car owner's focus and sources of information and inspiration shifts as s/he journeys on. Clearly, the brand experience, embodied in the car itself, the dealership and any direct contact between owner and manufacturer, is – or should be – a major influence in ensuring repurchase. The problem all car manufacturers face, however, is that models and owners' needs change, over the course of the typical purchase cycle, so that, arguably, *marque* loyalty needs to be achieved.

The table *(next page)* illustrates how different types of communication fit best into each stage of the customer journey. Within each stage, budget and creative considerations will dictate which are, in practice, used.

Schematic view of communication influences, by journey stage

Stage	1	2	3	4	5	6	7	8	9	10	11
Communication											
Image advertising	x	x	x	x	x	(x)	(x)			x	x
Model advertising					x	x	x				
Tactical advertising							x	x	(x)		
PR	x	x	x	x	x	x				x	
Direct mail	x	x	x	x	x	x					x
Customer magazine	x	x	x	x	x	x				x	x
Telemarketing	x					x				x	x
Website					x	x	x	x	?	x	
Promotion						x	x				
Test drive						x					
Finance deals								x			
Showroom					(x)	x	x	x			
Salesperson						x	x	x	x	x	
Print/POS						x	x	x	x		

A similar kind of decision process exists for financial services, especially where a branch banking operation is concerned. Here is an example from Abbey National.

The customer journey in branch banking

Abbey National's research showed that while customers were increasingly 'multichannelers', there was still a powerful need for a branch network. But the branches needed to change in order to provide a more welcoming, motivating and coherent experience. Abbey wanted to connect with its customers, and provide them with the right channels, at the right times and in the right way.

One outcome of the detailed lifestyle and observational research that went into developing the new 'convenience' branch design was the charting of an ideal customer journey, from initial attraction to the development of a long-term relationship. This vision was deliberately branch-focused, and used to identify the specific requirements of each area of the branch, as is shown in the illustration opposite. Based on this analysis, the bank was able to tailor the features of branch design and layout, the provision and nature of information and signage, the way in which staff should interact with customers, and so on.

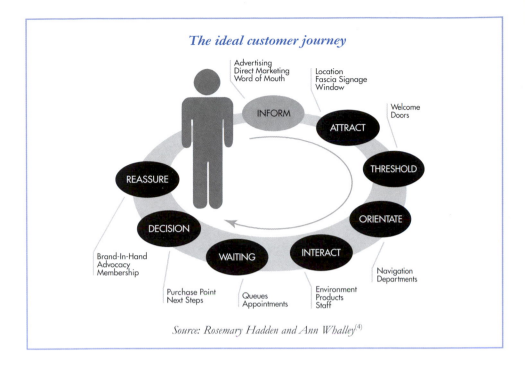

The ideal customer journey

INFORM — Advertising / Direct Marketing / Word of Mouth

ATTRACT — Location / Fascia Signage / Window

THRESHOLD — Welcome / Doors

ORIENTATE — Navigation / Departments

INTERACT — Environment / Products / Staff

WAITING — Queues / Appointments

DECISION — Purchase Point / Next Steps

REASSURE — Brand-In-Hand / Advocacy / Membership

Source: Rosemary Hadden and Ann Whalley[4]

Holistic Consumer Studies

Understanding the consumer decision process involved in buying frequently-purchased items presents a different form of challenge. There is often no conscious journey and the choice activity is much less obvious. How brand reputations are formed is also a less than clear process, depending on a mix of experience, perceptions and communications, many of which may be processed at a very low level, leading to *implicit* learning, learning that takes place without shoppers being aware that it's happening.[5] Understanding these consumer processes is fundamental to communication planning, since it will be vital to devise communications which will intercept people at the critical decision points.

These considerations have led to a considerable increase in the use of research involving direct, detailed observation of customers' lives and behaviour, whether instore (accompanied shopping) or in their homes and communities (ethnography). While these will not reveal how people are *thinking*, they get closer to the day-to-day realities of brand usage and brand reputation, or the actual use people make of media.

Two different types of observation study illustrate how they may lead to more valuable consumer insights.

Milky Way Magic Stars

Magic Stars were launched in 1995 as the first sub-brand in the Milky Way range, intended as a way of bringing young children into the brand. This meant that they had to appeal successfully both to children and to their parents, as purchasers.

Milky Way's agency, MediaCom, used observational research to develop strategic thinking which led to an interactive campaign which won a *MediaWeek* award.

Marketing to small children (and their parents) raises its own peculiar problems. For a confectionery product, these problems are exacerbated because parents are resistant to ads that sell sweets to their children.

Milky Way's Magic Stars campaign had a small budget – £150k – and was targeted against children under 5 and their parents. To develop an ad strategy, the agency ran an 'open day' for groups of parents and children, in a playroom with a wide assortment of toys and games and satellite TV. Observation of what went on showed that parents used a whole range of strategies to discourage TV viewing, and looked for educational, interactive activities with a good element of fun.

Based on this, the agency developed a communication programme built around carefully-selected children's comic magazines. The agency worked with the editors to devise an interactive campaign involving pull-outs, stickers and cartoon stories in the magazines, together with a series of competitions.

In spite of the absence of TV advertising, which is normally considered a must for children's confectionary, the campaign resulted in increased awareness and purchasing of the brand.

Source: MediaCom, based on MediaWeek Awards submission, 2001

Teenagers and the telly

An increasingly familiar genre of observational research is ethnographic research, where a team of researchers and a video camera enter the lives of a family, perhaps for several days, or even weeks, and record everything remotely relevant to the topic being researched. Understanding what goes on, and how it happens, can provide valuable insights for product and communication development, in ways which would be impossible through conventional survey or qualitative research.

The technique can be applied, too, to media, as the brief report below shows.

Saturday morning flicks

The Saturday morning stereotype is of a bunch of indolent teenagers sitting on a sofa in front of the TV, channel-flicking. Partially true: teenagers do channel-flick. They do this because they can, not just because they have the attention spans of gnats. It infuriates their parents. As we get older, our ability to hold different narratives in our heads at one time decreases, and the more we like simple story lines with beginnings, middles and ends.

But teenagers are far more sophisticated than being mere channel-flickers. We stayed with several families over a weekend to watch how they used the TV and other media. One group of three, two brothers and their sister, spent a morning in the lounge, segueing seamlessly between PC, TV and games console, plus a landline and mobile phone.

They acted as a collective rather than as three individuals, constantly talking with each other, sharing screens and swapping information. During this, they decided to go to the cinema that evening; and barely pausing from what they were doing, they checked what was on the local cinema via teletext, phoned by landline to confirm the showings and book tickets, then texted their friends to tell them the plans. The complexity of their behaviour and how they use different media simultaneously is stunning when closely analysed – something we could do because we had the films.

Another group, three teenage girls, played with a game, devising their own means of making it interesting for them but incomprehensible to anyone else. They used this to cement their relationship. To them, what they did was too banal to talk about.

Which is why we do what we do. Our research shows the ordinary things people do, day in and day out. Through close examination, we can view what people do, as opposed to what they say (or don't say). But the implications are profound – and a revelation to a client who had no idea of the complex mix of media her target audience was using.

Source: Siamack Salari, Everyday Lives Global

Data Integration

Good communication planning is knowledge-based. Nearly all companies have growing volumes of data from diverse sources: call centres, customer records, loyalty card schemes, promotion responses, email and website contacts, customer complaints, and so on. But turning that into knowledge that will inform multi-channel planning is a challenge.

Overwhelmingly, the biggest problem is that one source of data is almost never sufficient for all channel planning purposes. This means that the data planner must find ways of combining different sources and types of information to achieve a particular objective, be it targeting a mailing campaign or defining a creative or channel strategy. To devise and implement a complete campaign means that the planner has to combine and cross-analyse data from a variety of sources, which may be proprietary or in the public domain – customer records, TGI, survey data, media research, mailing lists (both internal and external), and so on.

To link data in this way requires a 'bridge' – common information (e.g. postcodes) or common analytic frames (demographics, media usage). The example below shows how one leading DM house, Claydon Heeley, approaches different types of data bridging problem.

The art of combining data

The use of a mix of data sources can provide insights for a variety of purposes. By way of examples, here are four possible types of data combination that could inform and illuminate marketing and communication decisions:

- Combining hard and soft data.

- Adding attitudinal information to a database.

- Linking media consumption data to purchase behaviour.

- Enriching a database with research.

Combining hard and soft data

Here, the base is 'soft' data, in the form of an attitudinal segmentation. This can be combined with hard data through the use of similar segmentations from public sources.

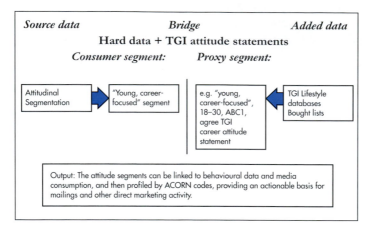

If we take the example of an attitudinal segment, the young career-focused, we could link this to the TGI by finding some proxies to bridge the gap. For instance, we may define search criteria as aged 18-30, income £15k+, ABC1 and agree with career-focused attitudinal questions on TGI. Having defined this target audience it is then possible to run the whole TGI database against the audience to see what other products they buy and what media they consume. From this information it is possible to see which brands (or third parties) index highly amongst the defined target group. Exactly the same principle can be applied to bought lists or lifestyle databases. This means that lists can be purchased, specifically targeting young career-focused people.

Adding attitudinal information to a database

Frequently, databases are almost purely behavioural in nature. A wide variety of material can be added to them, often simply by the use of the postcode.

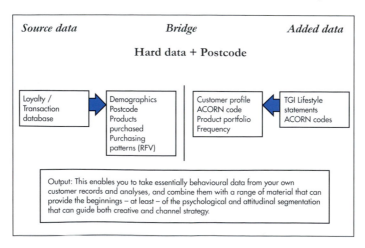

Companies with plenty of transactional data, such as retailers with loyalty programmes, utilities or financial services providers, are likely to have a loyalty or transactional database. Whilst they have plenty of behavioural data they may not have much attitudinal data to understand their customers. In this instance the postcode can form a very useful data bridge to access attitudinal information available in lifestyle databases. The postcode can access ACORN and MOSAIC profiles which describe customer types, such as White Collar Workers or Wealthy Achievers.

Linking media consumption to purchase

To identify appropriate media channels and manage their use, media research data need to be tied into information from other sources.

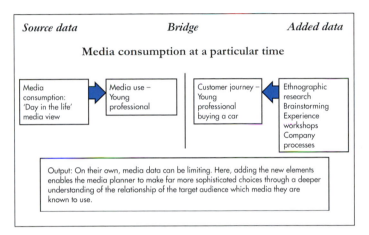

The data that can be combined here come from two different planning techniques. Take the example of targeting young professional first-time buyers for a mortgage. Media planners often look at a 'day in the life' of the target audience. For example, a young professional may take the train to work, read a newspaper, look on the internet at work, etc. This gives helpful clues to appropriate media to use. An account planner with a direct marketing background will approach the task through looking at 'the customer journey', which could be based on research or brainstorming. For example, someone looking for a mortgage might drive around the area where they are interested in purchasing a property, look in estate agent windows and search on the internet for properties before considering finance arrangements. At this stage they may approach companies with whom they already have a financial arrangement and speak to friends for recommendations. The data bridges are the links between the two techniques, such as internet sites with properties, poster sites close to estate agents or newspapers with property advertising.

Enriching a database with research insights

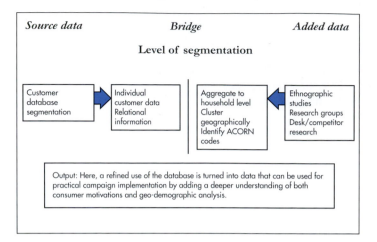

Many databases segment customers by high, medium and low value. Normally the segmentation is done at an individual level. However, research may reveal that it is more appropriate to understand customers at a household level or a geographical level. For instance, people in the same household using mobile phones often bought into the same network, as it was cheaper to call on net rather than off net. In appropriate instances, targeting by household can reduce mailing costs and increase efficiency by offering a loyalty reward for the whole household rather than sending four individual letters.

Source: Claydon Heeley

From knowledge to insight

Knowledge based on data analysis can only take you so far. Channel planning is an elusive concept which requires the additional ingredient of insight.

Clare Rossi of DM agency WWAV points out that if you are looking for insights from the varied data that DM databases can provide, it's important to have some sort of hypothesis about the type of insight you might find before you specify the analysis to perform and precisely what data to input. That way, you have a far better chance of getting something valuable from the process.

The sheer diversity of channel options, multiplied by the almost limitless range of executional possibilities, means that the process cannot be a linear one. Intuition and imagination are as important as logical analysis. Insights into channel planning require people who can process a mass of information, burrow deeply into what is known about the brand, its consumers, the media and the relationships between them, and out of this create or uncover the insights that will lead to effective communication programmes. A good discussion of what 'doing insight' actually involves is contained in an *Admap* article by Wendy Gordon, extracts from which are below.

In practice, what this means is that if you want an insight-based strategy or plan,
you need to be prepared to behave and react creatively, to use intuition and 'gut-
feel' to employ the techniques of brainstorming or creative workshops *(see page 47)*
to make apparently irrational connections and see where they lead you. And, as
Wendy Gordon says, be ready to share the insights you come up with.

For planning media neutral campaigns, the key is to work on the connections
between the consumer, the brand and the media or channel – the triangle referred
to at the beginning of this chapter. Making the links between the brand positioning
and its media context, and the ways in which consumers approach the brand (or the
category) and the media in which they expect or like to find it, provides a powerful
basis for the search for usable insight.

Insights can come from anyone. This has been recognised by the in-house
research teams of major advertisers, many of which have changed their titles to
include 'insight' in recent years, recognising that their managements rely on them
nowadays not just for data that keep them informed of what is going on in the
marketplace, but for proactive, creative and practical ideas – insight – to help drive
brands forward. The traditional categories have moved on: we now have data,
information, knowledge *and* insight. And insight is increasingly seen as key to
competitive success.

Helen Holloway, Marketing Director Consumer Insight and Communication,
Kraft Foods, describes Insight Managers as 'knowledge integrators', who need to
be able to orchestrate a range of information and experience of the company and
its brands so as to be able to supply the right information at the right moment to
arrive at insightful conclusions.[7]

In a panel discussion at the 2003 ESOMAR conference in Prague, two Chief
Marketing Officers, Patrick Farrell of Ford of Europe and Alessandra Bellini of
Unilever Central and Eastern Europe, together with clientside researchers Hans-
Willi Schroiff of Henkel K & AG and Arlene Pitts of Kraft Foods International,
covered the whole area of insight and what is expected of in-house and agency
Insight people. The quotations below illustrate how they approach the subject.

The role of Insight

[What we look for from our Insight people] is opinion, passion, judgement, prediction and prescription… The days when you could hide behind the data are already over.

Patrick Farrell, Ford of Europe

We see MR as the provider of integrated insights – pulling information from all sorts of sources and laying down a clear analysis of a very complex situation. The role of the consumer should be represented by someone familiar with the data, who is in tune with the life, the feelings, the instincts of the consumer…. In the end it's the consumer who counts. Walking in the shoes of the consumer is the key to the bottom line.

Hans-Willi Schroiff, Henkel K & AG

[We look to work with] integrated teams where the insight people are equal partners.

Arlene Pitts, Kraft Foods International

Our key issue is understanding the 'whys'. What lies behind what someone buys? We use outside agencies: internally, we have a very small team that works closely with innovation and R&D managers – as partners.

Alessandra Bellini, Unilever

Source: ESOMAR Congress, 2003, Panel discussion

At the same conference, David Smith of Citigate DVL Smith gave a detailed analysis of the role and nature of 'intuition', which, while not quite the same as 'insight', shares many of the same characteristics, and is a key part of the process. He defined intuition as 'knowing without knowing why' – a form of instinct or gut-feel – and he listed a series of characteristics of, and barriers to, intuition, which closely parallel those that can be found in relation to insight. These are summarised below.

Intuition: Characteristics and Barriers

Characteristics:
- Intuition can be cultivated. Practice helps.
- It is based on deep, organised reflection – as Louis Pasteur said, 'Chance favours the prepared mind.'
- It involves flexible, circular, not rigid and linear, thinking.
- It can proceed by 'osmosis'.
- It may involve either (or both) slow, gradual thinking and fast, instant conceptual leaps.

- It usually has a practical, as opposed to theoretical, knowledge base: knowing – instinctively – how to do something helps.
- It allows for ambiguity, uncertainty, imperfection.
- It is just one of several modes of intelligence (like emotional intelligence).

This is not far from classic descriptions of creativity.

Barriers:
- Flawed self-knowledge and over-confidence – we usually *don't* know it all.
- Lack of technical knowledge – so our intuitions are banal or literally impossible to achieve.
- Intuition may be a 'false friend' in dealing with uncertainty – we may base our thinking on misunderstanding or false assumptions.
- We may mistake lazy, simplistic, stereotypic thinking for genuine intuition.
- We are over-influenced by what is vivid, accessible, easy to understand.
- We can be misled by methodological bias – 'figure phobia', or over-reliance on statistics.
- We play psychological mind games which lead to false conclusions.
- Finally, it's no good having insights if they are not acted on. Failure to act is the ultimate barrier.

Source: David Smith, Factoring 'intuition' into the analysis of market research evidence,
ESOMAR, Prague, 2003

Insights, ideas and workshops

From all this, it is clear that insight is a creative process. By now, we have a wide range of experience of facilitating insights, and harnessing the abilities of groups and teams to develop them. The editorial team have compiled a selection of techniques they have found useful in workshops, both within agencies and client-agency, to help develop brand thinking and positioning.

One of the most enjoyable and productive parts of the process is when diverse talents are brought together to brainstorm ideas and generate insights. It's possible to move rapidly from the obvious to the fresh and surprising. Workshops are only as good as the people in them, and need energised and committed people. Including the creative people who will execute a campaign early on is also a good idea and bears fruit in the final result.

What follows is a 'menu' of workshops. These are all methods of questioning combined with a stimulus to creativity. They are organised in a sequence, starting with rethinking the fundamentals and ending with finding fresh ways to communicate. They reflect that most brands are in competitive markets and channel choice is a key part of any competitive strategy.

Mapping
What are the rules of the game in the category (or segment of the category under review)? Most categories break down into three potential positions:

- *The boss:* the leader in terms of market share, which usually owns or tries to own the most important benefit of the category and is more dominant in traditional media.

- *The fighter(s):* a strong contender which tries to define another way of leading in the category. Strong on differentiation, the fighter may have a different communications philosophy and/or route to market.

- *The rest:* perennial also-rans often play by rules set by the leader, but in a watered-down or less successful way. Face a dim future.

The exercise: break into teams of no more than four, work on the following questions and then debrief:

- Who is the boss and how did the brand become the boss?
- What is or are the boss's sustainable strength?
- What is the benefit the boss champions?
- How does the boss use media and other channels?

- Who are the fighters?
- How are they differentiated and do they have a sustainable strength?
- Does any brand have a strong alternative point of view on what should be the category benefits?
- Have any of them found effective channel strategies to side-step or outflank the boss?

- Play brandicide – imagine that a brand has been killed, suddenly removed from the market, and ask what we have lost that others in the market do not offer?
- Is it a practical thing or an emotional thing?

- What is the gap?
- Are there latent or emerging needs?
- Are there dissatisfactions that a brand can resolve?

Start Again
This is a good method of getting rid of baggage and getting clarity on a brand's distinctive offer.

The exercise: the company burns down – no premises, no production, no systems, just brand equity left. You have the resources to rebuild from scratch, thanks to your spectacular insurance cover. So what do you do, and how do you do it differently?

- What would you keep about the brand and what would you change?
- What would you keep about the product/service and what would you change?

- Who would your most loyal customers be – who'd stick with you and how would you reach them to let them know what's going on?
- Who would you target with your rebuilt brand and how? How would this affect your channel selection?

Revolution

This workshop tool builds on the previous two by looking at the assumptions and beliefs that are embedded in communications.

The exercise: revolution is about deliberately challenging rules and assumptions. The first step is to identify the rules that exist. Then take each rule, one by one, and break it. Each one offers the chance of a fresh perspective.

Once you've got your rules you can start to play around with them by asking revolutionary questions, e.g.:

- What if we did nothing?
- What if we had to make it for half the cost?
- What if people bought it for twice as much?
- What if we reversed the process?
- What if we exaggerated the issue?
- What if we hid it?
- What if we couldn't advertise?
- What if we couldn't afford broadscale TV? *(Source: ?What if!)*

Customer Journey

How customers choose and buy can be mapped as a journey (as outlined above). This can be quite long and involve several contacts before any purchase is made and is particularly true of high-ticket or high-risk markets. Customers use different channels to get in contact, gather information, view and purchase. There may be different journeys for different customers – having research on these can provide useful stimulus for the exercise, but is not essential.

The purpose is to:

a) understand what communications are optimal at different points in the purchase path.
b) analyse how the leading brand(s) use communications (the most traditionally effective media are often controlled by the incumbents).
c) identify gaps or communications that could be used to connect better with customers.

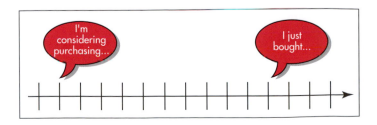

The exercise is built up in layers:

Layer 1: Map the different decisions along the purchase path.

Layer 2: Build a list of possible communication and/or contact opportunities along the path.

Layer 3: What are the moments of truth when reputation and sales are made or lost?

Layer 4: How do the leading brands use communications? Map these.

Layer 5: Ban the workshop from using conventional media channels (or that dominated by the boss). Does this lead to radically different approaches?

Barriers

If a brand wishes to grow it may need to attract new customers who would not consider it to be 'for them'. They may reject the brand, or it may just not be on their radar. Brands have barriers – real or psychological – that limit potential. Even if the brand objectives are not focused on new users, this exercise is useful because it can shake out any complacency that comes from studying regular or loyal customers.

The exercise: Identify the barriers:

- What do you have to do to restage the brand for new customers?
- How far do you have to go? Where and how would you have to communicate?
- What received wisdom about the brand do you have to abandon in order to do so?

Conclusion

Changes in media, technology, brand attitudes and society have stimulated brand owners, agencies and research companies to develop their own methods and processes. At the heart of these changes is the ambition to bring together the three elements of communications planning – brand, customer and media – so that findings can be of practical use in planning campaigns.

There has also been an increase in the volumes of research and data available to companies, which has led to a rise in the importance of 'insight'. Interestingly, the generation of insight is as much creative as analytical. People who can absorb all this research and data and bring instinct, experience and creativity to bear are increasingly valued because they make the complex simpler and more useful. They provide stimulus and focus to the multidisciplinary teams that create and implement the ideas for campaigns, which brings us to the topic of 'creative inspiration'.

Notes and References

(1) Professor Ehrenberg and his colleagues have argued – controversially – that most segmentation is pointless, since the demographics and attitudes of users of brands in a given category will show little variation.

Rachel Kennedy, Stephen Long & Andrew Ehrenberg *Competitive brands' user-profiles hardly differ* (MRS Conference) 2000

(2) For more on this, see Tina Kaye *Practical pathways to neutral planning* (Billetts/Royal Mail Media Neutral Seminar, Feb 2003)

(3) Louise Edwards, Ian Brace & Clive Nancarrow *'I hear you knocking …can advertising reach everybody in the target audience?'* IJMRS, vol.44 no.2, 2002, p. 193

(4) Based on Rosemary Hadden and Ann Whalley *The Branch is Dead, Long live the Internet!* (MRS Conference, 2002, courtesy of WARC.com)

(5) For a detailed discussion of low-attention processing, implicit memory, etc, see Robert Heath *The Hidden Power of Advertising, Admap* Monograph #7 (WARC, Henley-on-Thames) 2002

(6) Wendy Gordon 'I'll have one small insight and two large ones, please' *Admap*, Dec. 2002

(7) Interview with Phyllis Vangelder, June 2003.
See www.bmra.org.uk/mrbusiness/main.asp?ezine=101 for the full interview.

Chapter Three

Creative Inspiration

Janet Grimes

Introduction

Creative ideas are built on insights into people. At their very best creative ideas are surprising but true, get talked about, and not only stimulate short-term behaviour change but also affect long-term attitudes. In the total media age creative ideas are the vital glue that holds campaigns together and provides coherence and coordination.

Why coordination of communications matters

Put simply, coordinating the brand 'message' across communications channels and all points where the brand touches the consumer will typically improve the effectiveness of communication and therefore return on investment. There are several reasons why this happens.

Firstly, if a customer is using a variety of channels throughout the choosing and buying process, there is no choice but to coordinate properly. There are few things worse than a service brand that gives its customers a different experience each time they make contact with it.

Secondly, messages are not all actively processed. A brand that has a coherent approach to identity, messaging and tone of voice is likely to win the subliminal messaging battle by leaving a residue that feels positive in the minds of customers. In most categories, most of the time, customers are not actively involved in buying, but they will still be influenced by the communications they receive.

Thirdly, a strong central brand message, or 'big idea' (more of which later) will liberate different parts of the communication process to produce more creative ways of expressing the message. Multichannel campaigns are made by teams of specialists.

A strong coordinating idea can have a galvanising effect on the team, much as strong leadership can have the effect of getting a sports team to perform at its peak, with individual team members feeding off and energising each other.

Models of communication

There are almost as many ways to integrate and organise brand messages as there are brands but it is helpful to draw some general conclusions on models of communication, to allow communications planning to begin. The starting point is how customers think and behave, how they interact with the brand on every level, followed by the development of a communications model to fit the circumstances.

Most brands do not have the luxury of starting with a clean sheet. Having said that, a truly great, breakthrough idea which demonstrates a keen understanding of the target can revolutionise a brand. Sometimes it is a good idea to imagine that you do have a clean sheet. This is what Skoda did:

Skoda – a breakthrough idea that turned around a much-maligned brand.

During the 1980s the Skoda car was a joke in Britain. But at the same time Skoda went into partnership with Volkswagen and the results soon bore fruit, with the creation of the Felicia which won seven consecutive *What Car?* Budget Car of the Year Awards. Despite this, rejection figures for the brand remained fixed at around 60% over that period. Better cars were planned but it was clear that Skoda's image deficiencies would soon become a critical commercial limitation as it became apparent that the cars would have to compete for different consumers against a new competitive set.

The Octavia was launched in 1998 to great reviews. There was a £10m launch advertising budget and Skoda braced itself for success. But the launch was a failure. Why? The Octavia's marketing had been model-specific and product-centric, targeted at the small band of brand considerers; in short, Skoda was behaving like a brand without a problem rather than facing the truth and addressing the stigma.

New agencies were appointed in 1999 to plan for the launch of the Fabia, another great car that still faced problems despite becoming *What Car?*'s Car of the Year:

'I see the Fabia has been named "Car of the Year" but I don't think I'm ready to drive one yet. I still think that it's less embarrassing to be seen getting out of the back of a sheep than getting out of the back of a Skoda.' *The Mirror* – 26 Feb 2000.

The vast mass of Skoda buyers' friends, neighbours, colleagues and children could no longer be ignored – the target base had to be broadened. The two key strategic building blocks were:

- A new role for advertising: using the Fabia to confront the biggest barrier to buying a Skoda – the irrational prejudice against the brand.

- A new target audience: creating a general shift in attitudes so that potential buyers felt confident they could choose Skoda without being laughed at.

The resulting media plan was an old-fashioned broadcast plan. PR played a critical role at launch since press coverage was part of the problem.

The resulting creative idea has become famous. It repositioned the consumer. 'It's a Skoda, honest' featured people who still thought their cars were poor. By gently ridiculing these people, the consumer would conclude that he/she 'wasn't one of them'. The advertising changed the consumer's attitude to the brand. Key image measures improved quickly. The number of prospects who would not consider Skoda dropped from 60% to 42%. The Fabia relaunch was the start of an amazing two-year period for Skoda. The advertising and PR campaigns spearheaded a dramatically re-thought marketing programme that included innovative media thinking, new 'brand-led' direct marketing, POS and website, all catalysed by the change in direction.

DM, unusually, used a brand-led direct approach, adopted the advertising objective, strategy and tone and coordinated targeting, timing and creative. The first integrated campaign which ran from January to July 2001 decreased the rejection figure to 34%. The response was equally amazing. Response figures tripled, and for every £20 Skoda spends they now receive a quality lead. Skoda is now the UK's fastest growing car manufacturer.

Source: Archibald Ingall Stretton, Fallon and the IPA

What are the various communications models available to brands? There are no doubt many more than those alluded to here, but these models define different levels and types of creative integration.

The 'no integration' model

Although this is probably not best described as a model, in reality it is where many brands find themselves. Through history, the legacy of organisations, high turnover of staff – the reasons are numberless – this model occurs when the only thing linking the different communications is the physical aspect of the brand itself – the brand name, the logo and the product or service provided.

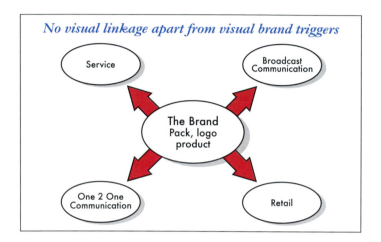

In some cases even the logo and the product can be presented in many different ways. So whatever is used in TV advertising may not be reflected in press advertising, and neither of these will be reflected in a piece of one-to-one communication. The service you receive may be delivered in a completely different tone of voice (the advertising might be gentle and sophisticated but the youth behind the counter could be surly and disinterested).

Why is this model relevant? It is important to know one's starting point, in order to begin to plan moves forward – and if this feels familiar it is because many brands are in this position. There can be advantages to having a completely 'disintegrated' model. Each medium can be used to maximum specific effect. Each message can be tailored to fit its surroundings. In other words it is highly flexible. It is a bit like the way local government was conceived– give the local council the budget and let it spend it the way it know best on the things it knows it needs. Actually, many franchise brands operate on this basis, giving franchisees some basic ground rules and then letting them deal with their own audience in their own way.

However, for mass market brands the disadvantages are also easy to see. Brand identity is quickly and easily diluted through lack of recognition. You have to start afresh with each customer in each environment and there is no cumulative effect of communications. Related to this lack of cumulative effect it can also be highly cost-inefficient. Taking a small step up should have big advantages.

Executional Integration

This has variously been termed the 'matching suitcases' or 'matching luggage' approach because while all may look very neat on the outside, it is possible that underneath the messages may not match up at all.

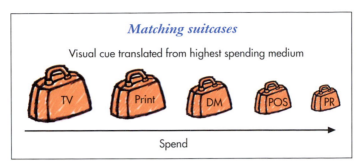

Matching suitcases

Visual cue translated from highest spending medium

TV Print DM POS PR

Spend

As the diagram suggests this is most typically used when there is one dominant medium of communications and at its simplest and commonest consists of a lifting of something visual which is then replicated in other media. This is mostly in the case of big TV advertising budgets but can also be seen in things like film, TV or books where a visual icon is carried across all communications. At its commonest a brand symbol (the Direct Line red phone, for example) is simply placed on each communications piece, whatever the message.

This can shortcut brand recognition. Indeed, it can create magnification of the core advertising idea when used cleverly. It also provides a level of visual consistency which can be less confusing for the consumer than the previously described approach. It can, however, get in the way of the message as consumers may 'assume' they know what's coming and switch off, denying the advertiser the opportunity to say something new. So use of this model should be carefully considered, and choosing the dominant visual cue should also be done with caution.

One example of the model's effective use would be the highlighting of staff in the Halifax campaign. Howard is the nice friendly face of Halifax, in some ways a replacement for the brand name. He is a mouthpiece for the message about 'giving you extra' and appears on most communications vehicles. And he has worked extremely well.

Halifax – Communicating like a Retailer

The Halifax case illustrates the power of an integrated communications idea to provide a galvanising and cohesive focus for a 35,000-strong personal organisation. It shows how a strong executional idea can cut through a crowded sector to produce an increase in sales and profit per customer.

In 2000 Halifax launched a commitment to steal market share aggressively from the big four clearing banks, through 'extraordinary growth in current accounts'. Important to this strategy was the need to create product substance in the form of a current account that paid 40 times better interest than the big four, and in the process to attempt to turn the current account market into a retail market that encouraged switching.

Key to this strategy was the need to communicate like a retailer, not like a bank by following the two key components identified by the agency:

- Focus on 'substance' in all communications – namely value.
- Using a strong communications idea to motivate staff.

Qualitative research revealed great pride amongst 'colleagues' in the building society heritage and a pride in being 'people not bankers', and amongst consumers in perceiving Halifax employees as 'people like us'. This led the agency to believe that focusing on Halifax as a 'human' organisation was a powerful platform.

The Brief:
The brand proposition for this campaign was: *Extra Value. Extra Friendly*, supported by *Extra value products – primary: current accounts; secondary: credit cards and mortgages*, with a requirement for:

- Advertising that is branded and cuts through immediately.
- Advertising that merges brand and product.

The Idea:
Staff as Stars: to use real Halifax staff singing their own pop video with an end-line 'Always giving you extra'.

Howard Brown
Halifax Sheldon Branch

Results:
Howard achieved 69% correct branding in its first burst and 76% in its second. The idea has proven to reduce acquisition costs. Click-through rates online are far higher than before for the same product propositions. The campaign's stand-out and appeal were similar to popular fmcg campaigns, highly unusual for the sector. Halifax immediately jumped from seventh position to first position on the shortlist of current accounts.

One of the most compelling demonstrations of the appeal of the communications idea is the breadth of uses to which it has been put. This is an idea that has been used organically by the organisation in a multitude of ways –

for recruitment advertising, in the internal magazine, at Sales Conferences, on the front cover of the Annual Report. The idea created more PR than any other campaign in Britain during 2001.

A single communications idea that fits all has saved significant internal and external resource by using the same concepts and photography for brand windows, product literature, conferences and presentations. It has been used in-store, in direct marketing, tactically and online as well as in advertising.

Sources: IPA, Halifax and Delaney, Lund, Knox, Warren

Brand icons and advertising symbols have been an enduring way to coordinate communications. Consider this list – the Andrex puppy, the Duracell bunny, the Tango man, the Marlboro man, the Oxo family, the Nike tick, the Lloyds Bank black horse, the Scottish Widow, the Esso tiger, the Strongbow bow and arrows. Apart from evoking recognition and affection, they are also valuable properties for the highly contemporary reason of media clutter. The puppy, the bunny and the Marlboro man were created at a time when mass tv ratings were more affordable than today.

Message or theme integration
A level beyond executional integration is theme integration.

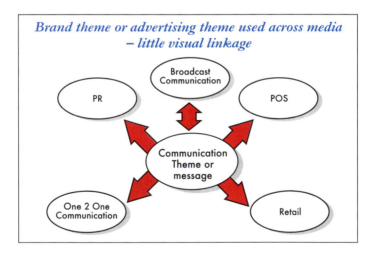

In this model, a common theme or message links all communications but they don't have to look the same – it is the 'take-out' rather than the 'put-in' that's common. It tends to cover only the communications planning so will appear in advertising, DM, PR and often at point of sale.

This creates a different set of pros and cons. On the plus side, as this model is centred around a message about the brand, and often the take-out of communication, it is operating at a deeper level of processing and is therefore likely to increase understanding of the brand positioning. This means the message is more likely to stick in the long term. The downside of this is that it can be harder to establish a message in the short term.

It allows channels to be used differently so long as the core theme is followed, and so each channel can be used to best effect. This approach is less likely to suffer wear-out as the clothes it wears can change, while the message underneath remains essentially the same. But it can be expensive and it can be harder to unpick.

Examples of this kind of approach are very memorable when used over the long term. 'Heineken refreshes the parts' springs to mind, and perhaps also the John Smith's campaign which, although it has taken three different turns, still communicates a similar 'no-nonsense' theme. Indeed, the current John Smith's campaign is itself a good example as it uses different creative mechanisms in advertising, sponsorship and POS but with the same underlying message. Stella Artois is another good example.

Stella Artois (Extract from IPA Effectiveness Awards 2002)
The advertising objectives have remained the same for many years: to encourage respect and reverence for the brand, making Stella the 'gold standard' amongst lagers.

The campaign idea has remained constant throughout the creative executions, namely that 'Stella is a lager of such supreme quality and worth that one will sacrifice something of value in order to drink it.' Likewise the executional formula has been retained (long time lengths, Provençal setting, timeless world, epic storyline, French language, resonant music). It is this consistency of advertising that we believe to be a source of its strength.

The media strategy has also been a source of consistency, contributing to Stella's ownership of quality credentials. Creative use has been made of a relatively low spend.

A programme-based strategy allows Stella to be present across the year and a focus on film as an ownable property capitalises on the cinematic appeal of the advertising.

Stella advertising has built, and continues to foster, a highly desirable and revered consumer brand. This has led to considerable direct sales growth and a very profitable return on investment.

Advertising is also having a demonstrable multiplier effect on the effectiveness and long-term value of promotions. Two elements of the marketing mix are thus working synergistically to create an effect greater than the sum of their parts, the 'Holy Grail' of marketing strategy.

What's more, advertising is still successfully communicating quality to an audience more and more frequently exposed to price-cut messages. Consequently the brand's premium credentials, built by advertising, have not been dented.

So Stella, a hero in the on-trade, is a hero in the off-trade too.

Source: Jo Reid, Lowe Partners Worldwide

Strategic Integration

On the surface this model has similarities to theme integration, but operates beyond just communications activity. There is a core brand strategy driving all the operations of the brand and this is evident not just in advertising, DM, PR, at point of sale and in promotions but also in the way the call centre operates, the product range that is sold and the way it is distributed.

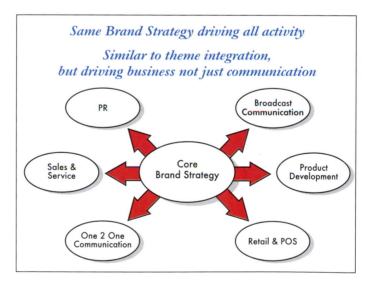

This model has strong advantages. It operates at many levels for the brand, moving beyond communications and into organisation and delivery, and is therefore highly credible for consumers. Whenever they meet the brand the same core communication about the brand is being transmitted. It is flexible and multidimensional in that the brand strategy can be delivered in many different ways. It can build both breadth and depth of understanding about the brand.

But, like the previous example, it takes longer and can cost more. In addition, it can often require organisational change.

A good example of this kind of strategic integration is the IBM e-business campaign, which became the catalyst for a major repositioning of the company and the business, stopping short of the next model of total integration only because the sheer complexity of the company meant its many services could never be completely integrated.

The 'Absolut' case outlined below could be argued to fall somewhere between theme and strategic integration, however given part of its objective is about product delivery, it probably fits better in the latter camp. It also demonstrates that clear definition of the problem can lead to better solutions and provide an opportunity for the consumer to engage with the brand in a new way.

Absolut Vodka Connections Case Study

In 2002, Absolut enjoyed a 50% share of the premium vodka market, yet only 3% of the total vodka market. The problem that faced Absolut distributor Maxxium, and advertising agency TBWA, was that the brand's communications were not engaging enough consumers. The root of this problem was identified as Absolut's confinement to the niche and fashion press, as well as its London-centric image.

A communications solution was needed to liberate Absolut. This meant the brand developing more accessible and engaging connections with consumers, alongside opportunities to try and purchase the brand. And it meant educating consumers about the attributes of Absolut and how to drink it. Therefore, a creative solution was needed that worked beyond the confines of traditional advertising.

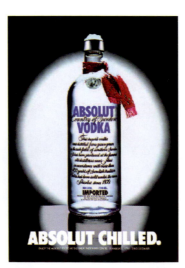

The creative solution was an event entitled *Absolut Chilled*, which took place over Christmas, 2002, in central Manchester, leveraging the product truth that Absolut is best served at 0°C. The centrepiece was the construction of an Absolut bottle-shaped igloo in the Deansgate shopping district – an area busy with shoppers representing exactly the audience Absolut needed to engage. The Igloo interior featured ice sculptures that recreated the appearance of a typical British living room stocked with a cabinet of Absolut. This was to reassure consumers that Absolut could be enjoyed at home too. And as shoppers walked through the igloo they were handed details about how to drink Absolut at 0°C and the bars that were promoting the brand.

PR was developed to raise awareness of the Absolut Chilled event and to encourage consumers to visit the Igloo. Coverage was generated in the local, trade and marketing press, online and on local radio. Outdoor advertising was used to generate broader awareness of Absolut Chilled in Manchester and nationwide. A 6-sheet poster campaign using a winter-themed execution from the Absolut catalogue with the headline Absolut Chilled was extended nationwide in the vicinity of Bar 38 venues. And a large-scale banner site was erected in central Manchester. Point-of-sale activity was developed to convert footfall to sales. Bar 38's windows were frosted up, leaving only the shape of an Absolut bottle. Inside, a snowfall was projected onto walls. And bar staff were provided with uniforms and incentivised to recommend Absolut and to educate consumers about how it is best consumed. Further ice sculptures provided sample shots.

Source: Neil Dawson, TBWA

Total Brand Communication
This model represents one extreme of the integration continuum, but while it may seem like nirvana it is not for every brand or service. However, there have been more examples of this kind recently as new brands are launched because it is easier to achieve starting with a blank sheet. More brands are also learning from the excellent examples set by the likes of Orange.

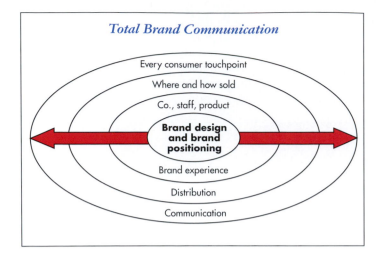

Total Brand Communication

Every consumer touchpoint

Where and how sold

Co., staff, product

Brand design and brand positioning

Brand experience

Distribution

Communication

This model works when the product, brand design, positioning and communications idea are in total harmony. One big 'organising idea'[1] provides the driving force for the brand. When you look at the brand from any angle, at any point, it is totally consonant with the positioning.

innocent is an example of a brand created with an idea at its heart which is translated truthfully in every area of both operation and communication, as this example shows:

Fruitstock – an innocent festival

On the UK's hottest weekend on record in August 2003, 40,000 people turned up in Regent's Park to a free festival of 'laidback jazz, funk, latin and hip hop', provided by innocent drinks.

It was a wonderful example of smart 'experience marketing', where the effort is towards deepening the consumer-brand relationship – in this case by providing a whole day out courtesy of the brand.

People could buy innocent juices and smoothies from the distinctive 'grass'-covered ice cream van *(see opposite)*, be amused by the company's other distinctively-liveried vehicles and enjoy healthy foods from stalls, plus champagne, Pimms, wine and beers from the bars. The many partners were chosen appropriately (like the Cycle London campaign, which distributed cycle maps from a stall, and brand partners like Ben & Jerry's, with their huge ice cream truck). And anyone wanting to be cynical about the motives behind the exercise was answered, as all profits went to a children's holiday charity.

Fruitstock is interesting for two additional reasons: how the event itself was promoted; and how the event was so completely in keeping with the tone the brand had adopted since launch.

The innocent publicity team call it 'innocent marketing' – entirely true to the brand. The advertising campaign for Fruitstock consisted of only three small press ads – two in *Metro* and one in *Time Out*. So how did the event manage to attract people in such numbers? The biggest communications channel was probably the bottle-labels, which since launch have featured whimsical snippets

---

of witty conversation and invitations to 'drop in at Fruit Towers' or 'call us on the banana phone'. At 25,000 bottle sales per day, the labels no doubt had a significant impact on attendance numbers. In addition, news of the event featured in the company's weekly email newsletter, which 3000 people have subscribed to, and on the website www.innocentdrinks.com and a dedicated site www.fruitstock.com. Conventional support amounted to a small amount of PR and those three press ads.

This is all in keeping with the brand's history. The launch story is an appealing one: 'Four years ago, we sold our first ever smoothies at another festival called Jazz on the Green in West London. It was the first time we'd ever tried out our recipes on the public, before we'd ever sold any drinks in the shops, and we set up our stall with a big sign above it saying "Do you think we should give up our jobs?" Under the sign we put out two bins, one saying "YES" and one saying "NO", for people to throw their empties into. At the end of the weekend the "YES" bin was full so we went in the next day and resigned.'

The brand's tone and corporate activities since then have retained the light-heartedness alongside a distinctive community responsibility – tree-planting initiatives and sponsored bike lanes in UK cities where their products are sold, and a percentage of profits going to support the community in India from which their mangoes are sourced.

At a time when many brand commentators are questioning whether people really want to have relationships with brands, innocent drinks received countless emails spontaneously thanking them for the Fruitstock event, and enjoys enthusiastic feedback every day by phone and email which it showcases on the website as part of the brand's appeal.

Source: innocent

The big advantage for this type of brand communication is that it provides complete credibility for the consumer. Everywhere they come into contact with the brand the communication is totally consistent. Another advantage is that money spent on the brand works quickly and goes further – brand recognition can be instant and almost visceral. For example, a piece of Nike communication has such consistency with brand tone of voice and positioning that the Nike tick is a piece of subliminal communication that evokes a whole set of meanings wherever it appears – even on a piece of armour in *A Knight's Tale*.

A potential problem with this approach is that it is very hard to build this type of brand communication for established brands, but not impossible. The Skoda example is a perfect demonstration of how real understanding of one's target can lead to a surprising and honest strategy that causes reappraisal. The Tesco case outlined below shows just how this *can* be done if the philosophy runs deep through the company rather than just the communications.

Tesco Case study – Why 'every little helps' is a great piece of glue
In the early 1990s, Tesco took some significant steps to move away from the 'pile it high, sell it cheap' image, common to many of its competitors, towards a more customer-focused culture and philosophy. The business defined one core aspiration; to create value for customers in order to earn their lifetime loyalty. In doing so, Tesco set itself a challenge on many fronts, by appreciating that 'value creation' could mean anything from low prices and good quality through to great product range and – perhaps for the first time – excellent customer service.

The acceptance of this challenge was articulated by the internal proposition 'no one tries harder for customers', externally encapsulated in the slogan 'every little helps'. This was initially evidenced by a series of one hundred new service initiatives, from bottle warming to one-in-front. These underlined Tesco's appreciation that even the smallest improvement in-store can have a big impact

on making shopping easier for customers. As further changes through the years have demonstrated, Tesco's equivalent commitment to quality, price and range, 'every little helps' has become a shorthand representation of Tesco's core philosophy – a simple reminder, both externally and internally, of why Tesco does the things it does.

'Every little helps', therefore, is not simply a tool for Tesco's communications; it extends much further throughout the many aspects of the Tesco business. Ensuring an 'every little helps' approach influences day-to-day operational decision-making and can help set the scene for longer term strategic planning. Equally, adherence to the philosophy behind the phrase is used to appraise individual performance, to evaluate the effectiveness of communications and to assess the brand image of Tesco as a whole.

Unifying and stimulating Tesco's communications
The challenges for Tesco's communications strategy are numerous. The messages conveyed nationally cover the breadth of Tesco's multiple 'fronts'. The predominant audience – Tesco's own customer base – is extremely diverse, so stories must be as inclusive as possible, to appeal to all. Add into this mix Tesco's local communications (new stores, refurbishments, etc.), the different media and the recent expansion into financial services and telecoms, and it would appear an impossible task to identify one unifying theme applicable across the breadth of activities.

'Every little helps' does, however, provide this theme, by placing the emphasis on the customer and the simple truth that small steps can make a big difference. In this way, a clear-cut principle has been set, namely that regardless of media or message, any Tesco communication should convey a genuine benefit to the consumer. This apparently simple premise establishes a definitive 'Tesco approach' across the breadth of communications, from POS materials in store to national TV campaigns. In addition, it provides powerful guidance for selecting worthwhile stories. For example, low prices are conveyed using examples and messages centred on *everyday* products; the benefit to the consumer is seen to be in spending less on the things they buy regularly.

As a result, 'every little helps' also stimulates creativity. Identifying and explaining a real customer benefit can initiate a different, more relevant conversation with consumers. This helps Tesco to stand out from the morass of standard retail communications. Where typically a new store opening would be accompanied by basic announcements, 'every little helps' pushes Tesco to explain exactly *how* the new store can contribute to making shopping easier for locals. Nationally, a full 'every little helps' press campaign has been built around conveying the different ways that Tesco tries harder for customers, covering everything from Tesco's Free-from range to 24-hour opening. Even trade-driving advertising, typically the domain of 'product shots and prices', has been aligned with the ELH philosophy through clear demonstrations of how the offers help in people's daily lives – feeding the family for under £10, a beauty regime for less …

The principles behind ELH also influence the creative tone; to convey a genuine consumer benefit with any credibility, messages need to be both empathetic and humble – Tesco appreciating that while it sets out to help, it is not the 'be all and end all'. Finally, the visual cue of the endline itself contributes to consistency across media and into store.

An operational and strategic guideline

Because 'every little helps' has become a means of articulating the company's core philosophy, internally it provides a consistently relevant sense check on whether the business is staying true to its values, regardless of growth and innovation.

Tesco's original focus on what helps make shopping easier has been retained. However, these days, this ranges from reassurance that the weekly shop will come in under budget, to getting a disabled parking space near the store entrance, or ensuring there is a range in store to fit most people's needs. As with Tesco's communications, continual questioning of 'where is the "every little helps" in this' ensures that new initiatives stay true to core brand values and maintain consumer focus.

Keeping things on track

Unsurprisingly, given their far-reaching impact within Tesco, the principles encapsulated by 'every little helps' also influence how the business is evaluated – for example, staff members are rewarded with highly prized Values awards, for incidents where they have gone out of their way for customers.

Equally, the broad spectrum of communications is tracked and appraised regularly against measures that establish whether helpfulness and a customer focus have been successfully conveyed. Looking ahead, there are ongoing efforts to ensure that Tesco's understanding of what is helpful to consumers stays relevant to the way their lives are changing.

A phrase encapsulating a simple philosophy

'Every little helps' is much more than an end-line or slogan. It started life as such, but has evolved into a powerful tool to maintain customer focus across business activities, unify otherwise disparate communications and create a relevant and unique conversation with customers.

Source: Tania Forester, Lowe Partners Worldwide

One problem with a totally integrated idea can be that it is very hard to change once established, but this is a problem many brands would gladly face.

A widely-acknowledged and oft-quoted example of a new strong new brand created collaboratively with a strong central proposition is Orange, as originally conceived. Indeed this has become the blueprint for many subsequent brands.

Orange case study – Extract from the IPA Awards 2000
NB: This case is from 2000 – changes to the strategy have been made since that time.

This paper puts the case for the Orange brand as a new form of patent – a unique and protectable form of competitive advantage in the new hypercompetitive economic order. The case shows how the ideas and ideology encoded within the Orange brand patent represent an extraordinary new engine of value creation for its shareholders – and an engine which truly transcends national borders. It is something which all would-be global companies should aspire to own. The future's bright, the future's Orange.

Orange has 34 competitors around the world in the seven markets where it operates. Orange is seldom, if ever, up against slouches. And yet it transcends them every time. The reason for Orange's apparently unfair advantage isn't magic, although it has something of the magical about it. The reason is that Orange was never conceived purely as a telecoms company. It was conceived as an ideology.

Source: Dan Izbicki, WCRS

Other examples of excellent media neutral ideas can be found in the 2003 *APG Creative Planning Awards* book (when released), notably that of Honda with its 'The Power of Dreams' campaign. This is the triumphant bringing to life of a real conceptual idea rather than simply executing it visually or single-mindedly – indeed, every execution of the idea looks completely different but demonstrates real 'Hondaness' in using 'The Power of Dreams'. The Johnnie Walker case is a 'masterclass' in how to take an idea and give it meaning in every part of the world in a true media neutral sense. And

Lynx – where an idea ('spontaneous dance') led media planning and execution down less traditional paths with great effectiveness.

The externally added value model

This is a development of more recent times and reflects what has happened in many consumer markets over the last ten years or so. Overproduction and retail competition have inevitably led to an escalation of promotions that sometimes add value but more often are thinly disguised price cuts. Researchers, particularly qualitative researchers who are in regular face to face contact with the public, are reporting that constant heavy promotional activity is changing the nature of the relationship between consumers and brands. Arguably, the consumer question at the moment of purchase is not 'which brand do I prefer', more likely it's 'what do I get if I buy you'. A factor in the growth of character promotions with properties like Harry Potter, Lara Croft and Disney is a growing realisation that for well-established brands there may be limits to the levels of brand approval that can be achieved through theme activity. In the externally added value model the importing of promotional values from outside the brand creates new reasons to buy, both emotionally, through the transfer of values from the character, and in real value terms, because there is usually an incentive that goes with the brand.

Promotions of this sort frequently use a wide variety of communication channels. Logically to get maximum value from the character association, the character promotion should intercept the consumer on as many occasions as possible and the character is the natural creative 'glue' that holds the campaign together.

Externally Added Value – Larazade: Lucozade and Lara Croft

The Challenge
To use the launch of the Tomb Raider movie as a chance to re-energise Lucozade's relationship with cult icon Lara Croft and encourage the youth market to switch brands and drive frequency of purchase.

Activities:
On-pack – promotional Lucozade packs were rebranded as Larazade. On-pack impact was reinforced with a two-tier Lara Croft promotion.

Off-pack – teams of Lara look-alikes on the street sampling and bringing the promotion to life. Plus a 'Lara' Capital Radio promotion and a consumer challenge on the Lara interactive website.

Other – included TV press and poster advertising plus POS.

Evaluation:
The campaign was measured in terms of sales (up 400%), the PR generated by the 'Energy Squads' and the participants in the website challenge (over 500 teams)

Source: The Marketing Store

Briefing for channel neutral ideas.

This chapter has referred to something called 'the big idea' or 'the organising idea'. The knowledge and insight section talks about thinking and processes necessary to drive towards a central brand positioning. This central brand positioning, or brand proposition, or brand vision – or whatever it is called – is an idea around which all brand activities should coalesce. While the proposition will be expressed in a form of words that is clear and easy to understand it may not always be expressed as an 'idea' as we have come to understand it in the communications world. Down the line, this can lead to many different interpretations by agencies.

Why is finding an idea, rather than just a positioning statement or proposition important at this stage? An idea is something that helps everyone that comes into contact with the brand to formulate what they see and think, in order to recognise the brand again – it is a form of shorthand, the way a brand looks in the physical sense (packaging, literature, product/service), the voice it uses with the customers, the promises that it makes. An example of a big organising brand idea is 'the future's bright, the future's Orange', which expressed the core Orange brand promise of innovation and optimism, but which was critically also built round a name, and a colour, directly connecting the idea to brand. It is something that not only encapsulates the promise, but encapsulates it in a way that makes it easy to replicate and recognise wherever it is seen and heard. A communications idea like this is a high-order idea which sits above different channels and which can be repeated or reorganised in a way that is appropriate to a given channel but leading to the same take-out about the brand by the consumer. It offers consistency and control.

It is important that we talk in terms of 'take-out' when discussing the big idea about the brand, rather than 'proposition' or 'key message'. A proposition or key message contains a specific offer, and can change according to circumstances, but take-out about the brand should sit consistently above this. This big strategic idea will be the springboard for executional ideas further down the process. These different executions within different media channels have much more specific propositions, as has been mentioned. So a piece of radio advertising with a specific brief to launch a brand promotion must give a specific message about that promotion but within the general umbrella of the brand idea.

Each discipline has developed its own way of working to meet the specific demands of that medium and will have its own set of briefs designed for that purpose. For example, understanding the digital medium is something which doesn't come without a great deal of specialist knowledge.

When it comes to the digital arena, particularly the web, repurposing offline ads simply doesn't work. Technological advances means that the web, and how it is viewed, is changing all the time. And not everyone views it in the same way. Any online campaign has to take into account that in any given target audience there may be people on slow dial-up connections as well as those using their office broadband. This has implications for the types of ads that they can see and how long those ads take to load. Photography, for example, takes a long time on slower connections whereas illustration is faster. Any animation or audio content can take time too.

Advertisers need to work out if they have enough time to get their message across. Remember, web users are active, they are seeking information and any advertisement needs to be relevant and entertaining enough to divert them from that journey. This means a number of things: Media and Creative working as closely as possible together from the beginning of a project; and being direct and upfront in any online advertising executions. Unless you have bought rich media formats, you simply do not have time to 'tell a story' or bury a product in the middle of an ad. The web has many unique qualities that can be used to good effect – interactivity being the main one – giving users the chance to engage with a brand and spend more time with it than perhaps they would by simply passive viewing of traditional media. Data capture and personalisation are also easy to build in. It is amazing how often campaigns fail to exploit these opportunities.

Source: Sebastian Royce – Creative Director, GlueLondon

This is great in theory, but in practice how does one increase the chances of having a great media neutral idea? One suggestion is that a media neutral approach needs a core media neutral brief, the purpose of which is to work towards the big organising idea. Once this idea has been agreed then it can appear on the core media neutral brief as a guide to all disciplines. Each client or big agency group will have a different kind of brief and this won't matter so long as it is agreed between all parties working on it. We would suggest that it requires the following elements:

Brand Proposition and identity

Agreed problem and goal

Key insights from thinking:
 Brand
 Consumer
 Channels

Desired brand take-out

Core organising idea
To be devised once the thinking process is complete

One example of this kind of brief was pioneered some years ago by MT Rainey, then of Rainey Kelly Campbell Roalfe.

Idea Brief

CLIENT: _____ **DATE:** _____

PRODUCT PROJECT: _____

This is a brief for a creative idea that's bigger than advertising and goes beyond advertising. In fact, it may never be executed in advertising. You may find you need to proceed to advertising executions to develop the idea, but the idea should ultimately be abstractable from the executions and be capable of being expressed in non-advertising forms. Or you may feel that the idea is intrinsic in this brief and you may just wish to concentrate on a creative or conceptual way of expressing this brief.

What is required:

Target Audiences:

Situation Analysis:

The Strategic Opportunity:

What is particularly meaningful about the company/brand?

What is particularly true about the company/brand?

What is particularly appealing about the company/brand?

Any other nuggets, thoughts, starters for ten or 'no-no's

Agency Review: Presentation:

Brilliant ideas are not guaranteed, but it will go some way to increasing the chances of coming up with an approach which is consumer-focused, integrated and which has considered all the potential options.

Source: MT Rainey

Improving the chances of having a 'big idea'

The key difference between channel neutral creative approaches and the old style of creative development is that no one medium should lead the others, but all should follow the same brand strategy and fit the brand idea. Executional separation between disciplines is still possible – and generally advised – but only once the central positioning is fixed and the central idea is mutually agreed.

Sounds simple. But the way the communications, and more specifically the advertising industry has developed has militated against this happening. Some organisations have recognised this and are taking steps to change the way they are organised to help change the way they behave. Here are some simple steps you can take to move towards a more cohesive approach.

Previously, much of the central brand thinking happened down the line, at the advertising agency, between planners and creatives and subsequently permeated its way back up to the client, and then back down to the DM and sales promotions teams, the PR people and the sponsorship people. This worked when budgets were advertising-driven but was not without its time pressures and political issues.

Channel neutral thinking requires a few simple steps. Firstly, decide who are the most strategic and creative thinkers. Secondly, form a team – this could be controlled by the client, by a third party (for example an agency brand champion designated by the client), or delegated to specialists. What is particularly important to success, however, is that the account planner(s) and media planner form a close working relationship. So long as the responsibilities are clear, and set out by the client (the alternative is a fight for supremacy), any of these approaches can work. Thirdly, the team develops the central idea that all parties agree on before any executional path is followed. This last part sounds easy but is in fact the trickiest. The following diagram outlines the vision of a media-neutral process:

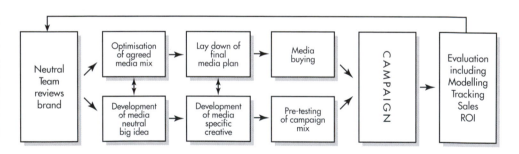

Source: Tina Kaye and Alan Wilson

Creatives generally believe that ideas are the product of their department and indeed they are best placed to generate ideas as it is their particular skill. However, creatives tend to think in terms of executions as this is how ideas manifest themselves, so trying to develop an idea outside an executional framework is difficult. It is doubly difficult in teams. No doubt new approaches will develop as channel neutral thinking develops. However, it is likely that those responsible for the core 'big strategic idea' will need a number of sessions, together and apart, in order to crack this idea. Structuring these sessions to get the best result is an art and may be made more effective by running the kind of workshops outlined at the end of the previous chapter. These work on the premise that good ideas come from anywhere and it is entirely possible, or probable, that an executional idea will emerge later on in the process that will improve on or even supersede the original big idea — every process should have the flexibility to allow for this and be alert to the possibility.

The Toyota case shows how an idea can come from 'left field'.

Toyota Corolla — a car to be proud of

The launch of the new 2002 Toyota Corolla — *a car to be proud of* — was a rare example of a big idea that didn't start out as a television commercial. Its very first execution was actually a launch stunt. People would cover their own cars with a special car cover that had the new Corolla printed on it. In this way they could pretend they owned one themselves. The idea went further still. It was proposed to place volunteers in crowds at football matches and other big televised events with huge banners proclaiming 'I've got a new Corolla'.

This exhibitionistic approach set the tone for the television and other broadcast media. We depicted people going to extraordinary lengths to associate themselves with the new Corolla. It was all about showing off and that is largely what broadcast media do — they show something off, big, bold and as public as possible.

Other communications vehicles encouraged greater participation from the viewer. For example, as sponsors of the BBC Good Homes Road Show, we invited people to use touch-screen technology to create their own *room to be proud of*. Similarly, we staged competitions at health clubs in which they could win a personal trainer for a year and achieve *a body to be proud of*. This was clearly part of the same campaign, but more of a two-way conversation with the respondent.

More playful still, we mailed prospects with a pack of *proud* prints — a set of stickers showing various views of the new Corolla that they could stick over their own car in their photographs to pretend they owned a Corolla too. Obviously, this takes the opportunity to interact with people at a more individual level. It's more personal than a broadcast message. It becomes more like hearing a joke from someone you know, rather than hearing it on TV along with the rest of the world.

New Corolla. A car to be proud of.

A nationwide programme of drive-in movies *(proudly presented by Toyota Corolla)* allowed yet another dimension to be explored – the first row of the audience was filled with new Corollas, allowing thousands of people to experience the car at first hand. Needless to say, the website featured the *car to be proud of* theme too, but here it was employed in a cleaner, information-orientated way.

Another idea almost turned *pride* on its head – working on the principle that the best way to create word of mouth is to ask people to keep something to themselves. Hence selected opinion-formers in the media and related industries were invited to a programme of 'confidential viewings' in the full knowledge they would tell their friends and colleagues and hopefully start a buzz even before the launch.

So the *car to be proud of* idea found its way into every conceivable communications vehicle but the way it was experienced varied from the more voyeuristic in broadcast channels to more playful and interactive in more personal one-to-one communications. In this way, we were able to harness the strengths of each medium, while still remaining true to the core thought.

Source: Adrian Zambardino, Saatchi & Saatchi

Collaboration is key to good integration and most clients will find that their different specialist agencies are increasingly happy to collaborate in the hunt for a good idea.

Start every dialogue with this question. "Does it have to be advertising?"

If the answer is yes, you're in luck. Advertising is easy. All you have to do is find a bloody brilliant agency.

If the answer is no, you're in for a lot of hard work. The supply chain management of brand ideas from client to customer can be as fearsomely complex as auto manufacture. After all, every client organisation has a different structure and culture. There's no one-size-fits-all process that guarantees perfectly milled channel neutral campaigns.

What will make it work are the people. Folks like these.

The client: the best media neutral clients are intimately concerned with return on investment. Rarely are they channel feeders or personnel managers of marketing departments. Their vision is to see the brand idea come alive everywhere.

The suit: on the agency side, the account director must think like a shadow marketing director and have a working understanding of the role of different media. Although they will have risen to their lofty pre-eminence via a single discipline, it is crucial that their agency train them in the many forms of marketing engagement. At our place they are regularly exercised at a sort of strategy boot camp. We call them "Spartans".

The planner: half account planner/half media planner, they represent a new generation of talent, often hatched in media planning independents like Naked and Michaelides and Bednash. They recognise the differentiating power of media selection and represent the consumer end of the ideas supply chain. Ambient, they are not.

The creative: if they are solely motivated to write 30-second sit-coms, best let them stay in their advertising silo. If they are unsettled working outside of the traditional writer/art director cabal, they probably lack the necessary confidence. Mould-breaking creatives are stimulated by working with colleagues from different executional backgrounds.

Only then, with this cast, do you stand even half a chance of having a genuine creative business idea.

Source: Mark Fiddes, Director of Creative Integration, Euro RSCG Partners

I remember reading in a book written by David Ogilvy in which he reckoned you were a lucky creative if you manage to come up with one big idea in your whole career. And he was only talking about television campaigns. These days we're expected to regularly come up with big ideas that will cover television, poster, press, below the line and digital and if it could have a spin off television show then that would be just great.

So how exactly should you go about finding one of these big elusive ideas?

Well, I don't think it comes from staring at a blank sheet of paper. Get inspired. Books, magazines, films, scrap books, your neighbour's layout pad. It's through looking at these that you build your confidence about what is right and what is wrong. Look for contradictions or problems. You can often turn these to your advantage. Stella Artois, an overpriced pub lager, has now become 'reassuringly expensive'.

Think graphic. Sometimes this can be the idea. The colour orange, for Orange. Prices and places in coloured circles, for Go.

Think tone of voice. Finding an original tone of voice that fits perfectly with your brand, can be a major breakthrough. John Smith's has been hailed for its creative campaigns for longer than I can remember, and there's been one consistent element all the way through, its flat-cap, no-nonsense tone of voice.

In these days of integration, there's also one thing you have to get used to. *You cannot do it all by yourself.* There's going to be a lot of expertise needed. Expertise you probably don't have. You're going to have to collaborate with outside partners, which means having the confidence to be generous with your ideas. You have to bash it around, argue about it, consider all the permutations and possibilities. Sometimes it feel like a shoddy compromise, sometimes it is a shoddy compromise. That's when you have to think hard about why you're doing all this integrating. Is it just about box-ticking? Will it really make better communications?

But the truth about being around big ideas is it isn't easy. In fact it's hard, really heard. It's the North Face of the Eiger. But that's the whole point isn't it. We wouldn't want it any other way. Would we?

So, get your crampons on and get climbing.

Kim Papworth – Creative Director, Wieden & Kennedy London

It is worth pointing out that media neutral thinking can influence every part of a brand's operation. Ideas do not have to be big central communications platforms to increase effectiveness. Thinking outside one's traditional silo and being prepared to think in terms of desired solutions rather than methodology can unlock the creative juices. Here are some thought-provoking examples.

Three examples of media neutral thinking – One and Three happened, Two didn't.

One: a particular segment was identified as persistent TV licence evaders in the UK. A group who, though it had the money to pay, would delay paying bills as a kind of game. The copywriter's suggestion? Send out a TV licence reminder mailing printed with red text, to mimic the 'final reminders' sent by utilities, credit card companies, etc. It's the appearance of red ink, he suggested, that gets these people to pay up. And he was right: it was among the most successful ever mailings to this group.

Two: the UK passport agency gets flooded by a wave of last-minute renewals every July and August, as people realise, with days to spare before their holiday, that their passports have just expired. Our suggestion? Rather than advertising, we suggested that UK passports were made to last a little longer than 10 years by a few random months, so that they did not mostly expire in the midst of the holiday season. They have yet to take us up on our suggestion.

Three: in the UK, the Directory Enquiries service was deregulated. BT wanted to promote their own 118500 service. We advised against simply advertising the new number in conventional media – 'People don't always call enquiries in the middle of an ad break or while reading the paper'. Instead we door-dropped 5 million of these little books of Post-It stickers (with 20 in each pad) to key areas in the UK. They'll have a far longer shelf-life than a conventional ad and, best of all, many end up next to the phone as a kind of point-of-sale advertising.

Rory Sutherland – Creative Director, Ogilvy One

Conclusion

This is a time of innovation in creative thinking as well as some traditional thinking being adapted for today.

We are seeing the persistence of some old models of communications because they are still fit for purpose. For example, advertising symbols are as old as advertising itself. They were conceived as recognition triggers for illiterate societies. Shopkeepers put out signs carrying symbols to represent their wares, and now they are recognition triggers that cut through the clutter of our contemporary media explosion. Advertising that is processed at a low level of attention often benefits from advertising symbolism. Think of insurance – most people don't, most of the time, which explains why this sector particularly values symbols.

Yet this is also a time of liberation. Arriving at 'big ideas' or 'organising ideas' is no longer something that just happens in the creative department of an advertising agency. Collaboration is vital and inspiring in both arriving at ideas and providing cohesion in their execution. The big idea that is 'owned' by all the people who contact the customer is much more powerful than one that is just handed down. Many brands today are differentiated by the conviction with which they execute their strategy rather than by any rational point of difference. Creative ideas are often the inspiration and intellectual glue that enable brands to create and sustain their distinctiveness and appeal.

Notes and References
(1) A phrase coined by Professor Angus Jenkinson in his piece
     'Integrated Marketing: radical ideas for a new vision for CIM'.

Chapter Four

Channel Planning

Peter Crawshaw

Defining Channel Planning

Channel planning is most simply defined as identifying the right mix of media to achieve your objectives. Before starting work it is essential to have defined the outcomes against which activity is to be measured, so that evaluation, which is the theme of the next chapter, can be designed now and not as an afterthought. Channel planning starts with this discipline; thereafter it is a blend of art and science with no single right answer. It is a collaborative process in which options are generated, assessed and optimised. Through collaboration commitment to a proposal is engendered, which increases its chances of successful implementation.

The key elements in the process are:

- An open-minded approach to consider all channels of communication.
- A clear set of objectives.
- Rich data built up from multiple sources.
- An understanding of the strengths and weaknesses of each communication channel.
- An understanding of how the channels interact.
- An understanding of how consumers interact with the channels and the brand.
- A prioritising of potential contacts.
- The development of theoretical communication plans.
- Testing, optimising and roll out of actual communication plans.

Channel planning is a creative process

As we said in the introduction, planning communications is like being an architect – all the correct calculations about materials have to be made, the building needs to be fit for purpose, and yet add up to a coherent whole which is greater than the sum of the parts. The making of a beautiful building is a creative process involving dialogue between client, specialists and architect, and so it is with channel planning. In the knowledge and insight chapter we provided some workshop ideas. These can be employed throughout the channel planning process to provide the stimulus for dialogue and fresh thinking.

Why brands use several channels these days

Using several channels is more work all round so why not just keep things simpler? There is after all no value in complexity for its own sake. The short answer is that, in general but not always, it bears fruit in greater efficiency and effectiveness.

- Research conclusively shows that harmonised, mixed-media communication is more effective in reach, targeting and consumer impact. Simply adding one more medium is likely to improve reach and effect by 10–20%.
  Professor Angus Jenkinson, Integrated Marketing, University of Luton

- The winners of the IPA Effectiveness Awards now use an average of four different media channels in their brand communications and the Holy Grail for all of us is understanding how to optimise that multi-media mix and prove its return on investment.
  Hamish Pringle, Director General, IPA

As media opportunities have increased, it is not hard to understand why a combination of communications is normally needed to achieve marketing objectives.

What is the right combination of channels?

Unfortunately for those who crave certainty there is no black-box solution, in which all the data and assumptions are fed in and the right answer pops out at the end. These models do exist and are useful as a guide or starting point. The options they produce are predictable partly because the assumptions inputed about the roles of different media are predictable too. Channel planning is not like a maths equation but is more biological, with multiple solutions that could work, some better than others.

This chapter guides the reader through a process that helps to narrow down the potential channel mix options, achieve clarity about expected outcomes and build confidence that a mixed media campaign will work together for greater effect rather than simply frittering away precious resources. It is above all a collaboration between different parties. The passage opposite, from NINAH, a marketing consultancy and part of the Zenith Optimedia Group, illustrates this point.

Thoughts on integration issues

When looking at what integration might mean in communications planning, there are three obvious areas to investigate:

- the creative and the message.

- the media planning, to convey that message and ultimately move the consumer to action.

- the client (the brand owner) and representative of the brand mirroring the creative and the promise.

Integration in communications planning, therefore, cannot be provided by the creative or media agencies, or the client, alone. An integrated communications planning process must be a process which brings together all these diverse elements of the brand marketing campaign – a process, which brings together the creative agencies, the media and promotions agencies and the client.

Increasing numbers of brands use this process to establish the impact of their brand investments in terms of additional brand value, short- and long-term sales and profit and changing customer attitudes and there are models to effectively support this.

Drivers include:
- Integrated communications often require planning across organisational boundaries, where an objective process can bring together business silos and media and promotional activity.

- Diminishing budgets require more sophisticated portfolio management. Reallocating budget between brands in a portfolio, or variants in a brand, has shown increases in profit in excess of 10%.

- Where good data is available, econometrics is helpful in understanding what has worked in the past, and it attempts to evaluate all communications vehicles in a single model.

Source: NINAH Consulting

The structure of the chapter

The chapter has four key sections. Throughout, there are practical examples and case studies.

The first two sections look at the properties and qualities of communications channels, which are the basic building blocks of a media neutral communications plan. Firstly, we survey the scene and then focus on the expanding areas of direct response and interactive. Before any combination of channels can be recommended, it is important that there is a clear view on the role of individual channels; we highlight the way that various communication agencies and clients view channels and their relative strengths and weaknesses.

In the third section of the chapter we look at the role of 'contacts' – a combination of data and channels. Using practical examples we show how you can better understand the effects of any contacts and how together they will help to achieve communication objectives.

Finally, we look at how you can start to blend these multiple contacts into an optimised plan.

Classifying Channels

Understanding channels

In the eyes of consumers not all channels are created equal. There is a multitude of ways of classifying channels and here we show how these have been used to produce more effective communication campaigns. Through looking at the ways channels could be classified the aim is to create a 'map' of the landscape enabling better understanding of how channels can work together.

The CRAM International classification

CRAM International, a qualitative research company, looked at the ways in which consumers get involved emotionally with different channels at a high level. The channels researched via qualitative groups were Letters/Mail, TV, Outdoor, Print and Internet. What is clear is that there are large differences in the ways in which these channels are processed and the mood consumers tend to be in when interacting with them.

As can be seen from the table below, measures like intrusiveness, attention span mood and context vary greatly and produce very different responses.[1]

COMPARISON OF MEDIA PROPERTIES

	LETTERS/MAIL	TV	OUTDOOR	PRINT	INTERNET
Intrusiveness	Very high	High	High	Low	Low
Episode attention span	Long (letters) Short (mail)	Long	Short	Long	Restless, fragmented
Control/selectivity of consumption	Passive at point of contact	Passive	Passive	Active, selective	Active, selective
Active processing	Highly active, Focused	Low	Low	High	High
Mood	Hope/longing seeking excitement Mail: suspicious sceptical	Relaxed, seeking emotional gratification	Bored, under-stimulated	Relexed Seeking interest / stimulation	Goal orientated Needs related
Modality	Visual some tactile	Audio/visual	Visual	Visual	Visual (auditory increasing)
Processing	Semantic Deep (letters) Superficial (mail)	Episodic Superficial	Episodic / semantic	Semantic Deep	Semantic Deep
Context	Individual Private Some sharing	Individual in interpersonal setting: Sharing	Solitary (in public space)	Individual Personal	Alone Private

Interestingly, even within channels there are differences. For example, personal correspondence is treated differently from mail from organisations. And mail from an organisation that a person is familiar with receives much more attention than that from an unknown source.

CRAM International plotted media benefits, collected via research, on a graph that looked at the level of emotional involvement and its 'durability'. TV or cinema ads are *involving* because they are active and dynamic. However, their transient nature requires either frequency or dramatisation to implant a message. There are commercials that you only need to see once for them to be remembered but these are few and far between. Mail, on the other hand, is a physically tangible and durable communication. Leaflets can be reread and stored as an aide-memoire, as can websites, especially when stored in the Favourites file. They can also carry more complex messages and detailed information.

On an emotional level media have different properties. TV uses the dynamic nature of moving pictures, music and sound for attention and impact. Mail can use more of the senses – visual, touch, taste and smell – for a richer communication. The web can make consumers feel in control.

These classifications are useful because they both suggest ways of putting channels into complementary combinations and stimulate ideas for innovative use of channels. For example, new technology means that both cinemas and mail might be ways to experience the fragrance of a new product.

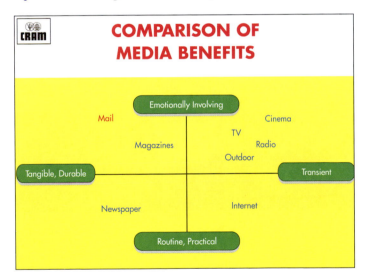

How might this matrix be used to channel choice? If you can encapsulate your message in a simple visual then the outdoor medium could be very appropriate; if you need to impart a lot of information then a print medium could be effective; if you want slow seduction then magazines might be right. Finally, the matrix enables a picture to be built as to how each channel might play a complementary role in a multimedia campaign.

Whiskas – CASE STUDY

Whiskas capitalised on the high levels of emotional involvement and durability the mail channel can have when they moved from TV advertising to mailing samples to boost the penetration of the Whiskas cat food in pouches.

Whiskas – navigate the best way to the consumer

Agency   PHD

Client   Mars Petfoods

Situation   18 months after a classic FMCG launch (heavyweight national TV and discrete sampling) of Whiskas new 'pouches' penetration had stalled.

Objective   Regain brand's No.1 position.

Insight   Trial is key with owner agreement that 'Cats choose their own food' The new pouch format allows novel ways of delivery.

Campaign   Rather than use the classic push approach of TV, Whiskas changed to a more involving strategy. The pouch format allowed direct mail to be used to deliver 6 packs of food to over 1.5 million households. The pouches came with a feeding diary to generate involvement and data. TV and Radio were used to support the DM work.

Results   20% uplift in sales after only 14 weeks. 73% increase in penetration. Brand reclaimed No.1 position and could claim 90% of cats prefer Whiskas.

Chrysler – Building a Pre-launch Customer Base

Agency	Langham Works
Client	Chrysler Jeep UK
Situation	The Chrysler Crossfire faced a pre-launch communications challenge to maintain interest in the Crossfire in the face of multiple rival launches, and convert it into sales.
Objective	Sell 400 cars. To achieve this, Chrysler needed to protect early deposit-paying customers from competitive launch activity, build a prospect pool and persuade prospects to place an order – before the actual car launch.
Insight	Using multimedia communications, customers can be nurtured through an extended pre-launch period through the use of exclusive updates on the product. An 'ownership' experience can be developed even without the benefit of the product itself. This approach must be built on a solid platform of customer understanding.
Campaign	The emphasis for deposit payers was reassurance of the purchase decision, maintaining commitment and passion. Following the theme 'More details to follow', the five-stage campaign was led by high quality direct mail, collected into the special integral metal box by the customer. It focused on keeping them informed well ahead of the public and culminating in invitations to exclusive viewings of the vehicle. Emails linked to a closed microsite were also used, plus a DVD showing the Crossfire on the road. The final element communicating the launch event date included

an offer of a Crossfire-specific advanced driving programme from the Institute of Advanced Motorists.

The prospect pool was built primarily through extensive press coverage of the Crossfire, all of which drove prospects to the Chrysler Crossfire website where they registered for the campaign. A questionnaire on the website allowed Chrysler to build detailed profiles. The prospect campaign used email linked to another closed microsite for its main thrust, providing information on the car slightly behind the deposit-payers programme (still ahead of general release). All communications stressed the need to reserve a car with a deposit to be sure of owning one of the limited first-production run.

Results   The campaign objective of 400 unit sales was beaten by well over 50%, selling out the entire UK production run and meeting Chrysler's business objective of a full order bank for the launch. Production has now been increased to meet demand.

Classification of communication channels by their power to influence behavioural change

Naked, a communications planning company, classifies communication channels by the power they have to influence consumer behaviour.

Naked sees four types of channel that can be used to build meaningful communications with people. The channels in the higher dimensions are more influential in changing consumers' behaviour and while some of the higher dimension channels can be harder to control they can have effects well in excess of the on-paper spend.

- The 1st dimension is one-way advertising. (TV, press, radio, cinema, posters.)

- The 2nd is two-way dialogue; channels when a relationship can be built. (DM, internet, telephone.)

- The 3rd is the 3D experience, where a consumer can touch and feel a brand, and where a deeper relationship can be built. (Road shows, test drives, free samples.)

- The 4th dimension is classified as viral; this is the most powerful, in that it is one where word-of-mouth and brand ambassadors are created. (PR, viral marketing, communities of interest.)

Looking at media channels according their ability to influence the behaviour of the consumer can lead to novel ways to use media. Also, understanding the power of individual media influences how the messages are deployed.

Naked identifies all the possible communication channels and classifies them. It then creates communication plans that not only use multilevels but, where possible, involve 4th dimension media – the most powerful and most influential.

Batchelors Supernoodles

The use of combined levels of contact, and a 4th level medium is shown in the work Naked did with Batchelors 'Supernoodles'. Through combining late-night TV and Vindaloo blast zones in selected pub toilets, they created very high levels of awareness and discussion in the target market resulting in a lot of PR, word-of-mouth and sales.

O_2 picture messaging – CASE STUDY

In a similar approach the communications agency VCCP created groups of picture message users (in effect a 4th dimension media channel) to become the evangelistic users of this new way of communicating.

Driving up the usage of picture messaging

Agency	VCCP
Client	mmO_2
Situation	Multi Media Messaging or MMS was the telecoms marketing story of 2002. All the mobile operators, apart from O_2 had launched an mms service. In combination the millions of pounds spent by O_2's competitors meant that awareness of the technology was high but actual usage was very low. Advertising generated awareness had not led to behaviour change.
Objective	To use a budget that was modest by industry standards to drive usage rather than to further inflate awareness of the technology.
Insight	To achieve significant take-up MMS had to get into the hands of the most frequent texters, (under-35s) and had to become part of their everyday text habit.
Campaign	First, VCCP worked with O_2 to use call pattern data to identify groups of young people who called and texted each other frequently and to isolate the individuals within these peer groups most likely to instigate communication between the group. By inference, these individuals could be assumed to be the dominant influencers within the peer group.

These individuals were recruited via a research company to attend a briefing at which they were given an MMS-enabled handset, a |

preferential tariff for mixed media messages and instructions as to how to send such messages. Their call pattern and the impact on MMS adoption amongst their peer group were monitored closely for the following three months.

Second, VCCP developed a campaign idea that positioned MMS as part of the language of text. The 'invent your own language' idea demonstrated how pictures could further improve the ability of text to short code everyday messaging between friends.

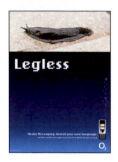 

Third, VCCP developed this idea into a fully integrated campaign using media ideally suited to impact upon the under-35s audience at the very time when they were out and about, using sms and therefore most likely to recognise the relevance and appeal of MMS.

Results   The seeding programme alone achieved significant returns for O_2. Within three months there was a near 40 per cent growth in the penetration of MMS-enabled handsets amongst those who were in contact with one of the original seeds. Aside from the seeding programme, general tracking showed that, by the end of 2002, O_2 had achieved MMS usage levels amongst the crucial under-35s audience that were significantly higher than those achieved by its far higher spending competitors, Vodafone and Orange.

The Diageo way – segmenting channels by brand relationship

Returning to the Diageo way of brand building introduced in Chapter 1 (page 26), below is a typical channel planning grid that shows how a task is broken down by consumer group and channel suitability. As can be seen from the table below experiential marketing channels can have very different effects on conversion for *Adorers* and *Availables*. With *Adorers* they reinforce positive brand benefits, for *Availables* they are simply offering a low-risk way of trying.

Channel selections and their desired effects (Extract)

Note: Where no role is shown, this channel would not be a first choice to achieve the desired conversion effect.

	Adorers	**Available**
Desired conversion effect	Increase frequency of brand choice	Encourage trial
Advertising	–	–
Experiential Marketing	Engaging experiences with new content or in new environments that reinforce positive brand beliefs	Opportunities for low-risk trial in relevant environment
Consumer PR	–	–
Relationship marketing	Customising products, offers, information and or services	Provision of direct incentives to trial

Understanding how a consumer relates to your brand is an important factor in deciding which channels will be most effective in communicating with them.

Additionally, Diageo views the road between problem and solution as littered with barriers. These barriers are identified in an insight planning stage and importantly they are addressed in the channel selection stage.

Guinness – CASE STUDY

This case shows how identifying the barriers can stimulate lateral solutions. Guinness was looking to increase conversion rate in the Availables group so was looking for the best opportunities of low-risk trial. Insights from field research led to a change in approach.

Using research insight to overcome barriers to ordering Guinness in a pub environment

Client Diageo

Situation Few people love Guinness on first tasting. However, after a pint or two, few can resist its charms. Guinness used to address this key barrier by taking interested drinkers away for an exclusive evening. However, back in the pub with their mates, they still didn't order Guinness.

Objective   Increase the sales of Guinness in a pub environment.

Insight   Further field research showed this was down to the physical issues of waiting to get the pint and consequently missing out on the key first few minutes of bonding with the group.

Campaign   Having identified the barrier it was clear that Experiential Marketing would be a more suitable channel to use than, for instance, advertising or PR.

Guinness in fact took two approaches to address these new barriers: it now only takes whole groups out for evenings with Guinness, looking to persuade the whole group to drink Guinness, so they now bond while they are waiting for the pint to settle.

Product Innovation – finding ways of producing a pint a lot quicker.

Results   The Experiential Marketing approach has proved very successful and is being applied in several countries.

Classifying channels by the product adoption curve – CASE STUDY
We introduced the product adoption curve and its implications for channel selection in Chapter Two. The launch of the MINI shows how using the adoption curve model can produce innovative and distinctive use of channels during the different phases of brand or product adoption.

MINI – targeting media to product life cycle

Agency   WCRS

Client   MINI

Situation   Launching a new car with an incredible heritage on a limited budget.

Objective   1) Use media to demonstrate MINI as a brand that bucks convention.
2) Use media to celebrate MINI's personality.

Insight   The adoption curve is a well-used tool. However, a typical car launch involves a blockbuster 60" TV ad supported by double-page spreads in the Sunday supplements and perhaps a large burst of outdoor. Does this effectively target the people who are seen as the innovators?

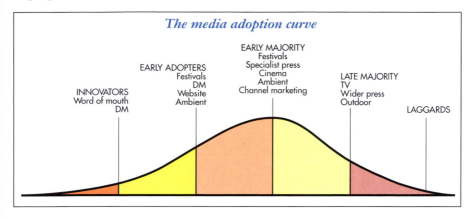

The media adoption curve

INNOVATORS
Word of mouth
DM

EARLY ADOPTERS
Festivals
DM
Website
Ambient

EARLY MAJORITY
Festivals
Specialist press
Cinema
Ambient
Channel marketing

LATE MAJORITY
TV
Wider press
Outdoor

LAGGARDS

As early as 6 months before the launch, ambient media was being used for MINI to encourage the innovators and early adopters to take notice. It was imperative to start getting the people who influenced and moulded opinion to talk about MINI and begin to re-establish the brand's iconic status. MINI's guerrilla agency, Cunning Stunts, delivered a campaign which sought to reacquaint the British public with the MINI personality, without revealing the main thrust of communication. Undercover promotional teams were sent to hotspots around the country and employed to slip hand-written messages on matchbooks to people they thought suited MINI or leave packets of saucy MINI photographs on tables to be discovered.

The campaign moved on to targeting the early majority through cinema and the style press and eventually the late majority through TV and a wider press schedule.

Results   By the end of 2002 MINI had achieved a market share of 2.04% and had exceeded its sales targets by 21%. The cinema campaign achieved the highest ever-recorded Total Recall score.

Classifying channels around the 'Brand Story'

Circus, which defines itself as a Brand Engagement® company, has classified channels by their usefulness in telling 'a brand story'. They see all communications fitting into four classifications:

- Voice of the brand – what the brand communicates to the consumer.
- Place of the brand – where a consumer can interact with the brand.
- Behaviour of the brand – what people who work for the brand say and feel about it.
- Offer of the brand – how the brand experience is delivered.

Voice: advertising (press, outdoor, radio, TV, cinema), PR, graphic design/identity, face-to-face (door-knocking), stunts, language/symbols, direct mail/print, digital. (broadly, everything that sits within the marcoms arena).

Place: architecture/interior design, work environments/head offices, retail space/presence, touring/brand experiences (such as Legoland), internet presence (for some clients this comes under Voice – depending on business use of the internet), and exhibitions.

Behaviour: internal culture (internal communications/management style), HR policies and practices (such as recruitment – additional team members to support a launch, appraisals, individual targets/appraisals, training), environmental policies, corporate and social responsibility.

Offer: products and services, channels (retail, mail order, etc.), pricing (for example; promotions tailored to campaigns), fulfilment.

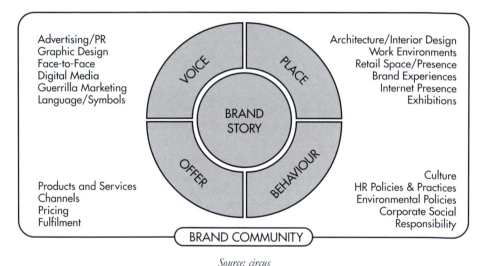

Source: circus

Floodline – CASE STUDY
The Floodline example shows how Voice, Offer and Place were combined to good effect.

Agency	circus	
Client	Floodline	
Situation	Develop and deliver a 10-year public flood awareness campaign.	

Objectives	•	raise awareness of flooding, particularly among people living and working in flood risk areas.
	•	encourage individuals to take practical steps to prepare for flooding to clarify the role of the Environment Agency in flood warning and offering support to the public at risk.
Insight		Put the people at risk at the centre of all communications and use a consumer (not a technical) tone of voice.
Campaign		A sub brand 'Floodline' was created, which is central to all communication elements.

PR – After introducing a new set of warning codes the BBC was persuaded to include them in the weather forecasts.

Local level activities included events, posters and direct mail targeted to flood risk areas and storylines in *The Archers* and placing material in *Hollyoaks* and *Brookside*.

Results	•	Since launch in 1999, Floodline has received over 1.5 million calls.
	•	98% people at risk now agree that 'flooding is a serious issue'.
	•	72% of people at risk are now aware that they live in a flood-risk area.
	•	83% of people at risk are aware (spontaneous and prompted) of the Agency's role in flooding.

84% (versus 57% in 2000) of people at risk can think of precautions they should take.

Innovative direct mail items have helped ensure that, among those mailed, 75% of people have kept items such as warning code and Floodline wallet cards.

Classifying direct response channels

Experian, a data analysis and direct response company, focuses on how to classify the burgeoning number of direct response channels. The full report can be found at www.growmorebusiness.com/media.html. With each direct channel Experian simply lists strengths and weaknesses. However, even with this simple approach huge differences are evident.

Experian's view of direct marketing channels

Channel	Strengths	Weaknesses
Direct Mail (DM)	The highest level of targeting with advantage of being discrete	Expensive and can have junk mail image
Telephone – inbound	Acceptability and good for collecting additional information	Cost (especially if Freephone) plus hidden training costs
Telephone – outbound	Can tailor message during call, can be highly responsive	Intrusive and can be very damaging if done badly
DR –TV	Large potential audience, rapid response	High overall cost, poor targeting, low quality response
DR – Radio	Surprisingly affordable, good for local targeting, cannot convey detail	Needs constant repetition and not good for complex messages
National newspapers	Large audience, short lead time	Cost, short life, poor targeting
Specialist magazines	Good targeting, long life	Longer lead times, extra costs of production
Door-Door	Can deliver samples and cheaper than DM with some targeting	Seen as junk
Inserts	Very responsive, can convey detail	Costs 3–5 times a page ad with longer lead times
Fax mailings	Cheap and fast	Poor quality output and can get lost in office environment
Email	Cheap fast and increasingly targetable	Spam, and businesses increasingly don't accept attachments
The Internet	Cost-effective and fast to implement	Not cost-effective for non e-commerce site

Experian's work is a useful corrective to an oversimplistic view of direct response advertising. Different direct response channels have different qualities and characteristics. Imaginative combinations are possible.

Matching up communications objectives to channels strengths will undoubtedly increase the effectiveness of any communications. Equally being aware of any weaknesses can ensure they are addressed in other areas, i.e. the creative side of executions.

BT broadband – CASE STUDY

Matching a channel's strengths to a key communication objective is seen in the BT Together Local launch case study, where the stealth power of direct mail was used to launch a new product first to selected valuable and vulnerable existing customers. The subsequent heavyweight ATL campaign then served to remind those 'selected' customers that BT had chosen to tell them first, thereby building a stronger relationship with those individuals.

BT Together Local
Addressing customer loyalty in a new product launch

Client	BT – BT Consumer Division
Situation	BT was about to launch a package customers really wanted – free local calls. The product had been well received by customers in research and needed a big campaign idea to maximise the product.
Objective	To use the launch of BT Together Local to strengthen the relationship that valuable and vulnerable customers have with the brand while still meeting tough sales targets.
Insight	In research groups customers often said 'BT aren't going to do this, are they? If they did I'd tell all my friends.'
Campaign	DM was used to introduce the product to selected customers. The campaign was then broadened out using TV, outdoor and press. The weight and scale of these subsequent media helped reinforce the personal nature of the first mail piece.
Results	The campaign had very high response rates, great sales and perhaps, most importantly, calls from customers who didn't even receive the mailing. Hence customers were doing the marketing for BT. A telephone tracking study also showed that customers who received the mailing (both responders and non-responders) had significantly higher brand scores than the control cell. The strategy was used again in 2003 for the launch of BT Together UK.

Classifying and understanding the internet

The internet is still a relatively new and powerful medium that is changing as we watch. However, unlike many other media it has already been used in many different ways, and the list grows. As it becomes more important, understanding the various ways it can be used is vital. Zed, the interactive arm of Zenith Optimedia, like Experian, takes the classification of different channels to the next level by focusing on the many ways you can communicate with consumers via the web.

As can be seen from the charts below, according to Zed research the many types of advertisement possible on the Internet are perceived very differently by consumers, with superstitials being most similar to TV and buttons and banners having more similarity with direct mail. In addition the response rates vary enormously, as can the cost per thousand to produce them.

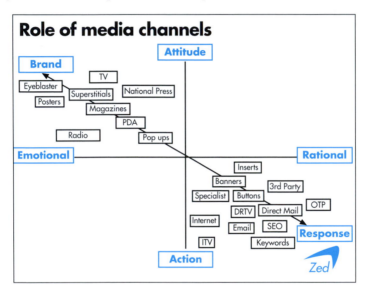

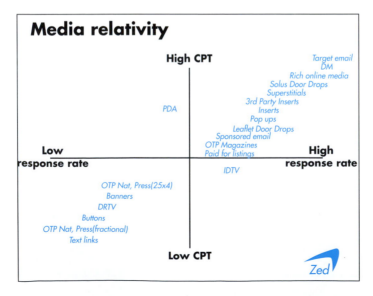

THE COMMUNICATIONS CHALLENGE

Combining hard data, soft data and judgement

In Chapter Two we discussed how data could be fused together via data bridges to generate insights. Here we review two different approaches for bringing together hard and soft data with creativity and knowledge.

First, let's look at Naked, which uses commercially available data (TGI, for example, in the UK) and a relatively simple, sometimes subjective, process to make intermedia comparisons. This approach is quick to apply and very inclusive.

The quantitative approach it developed is called 'Selecta'. It uses syndicated lifestyle data (in the UK BMRB's TGI works effectively), and involves creating a target or a series of target group consumers and then determining the efficiency and effectiveness of channels spanning each of the four dimensions of available communications.

Step 1: looks at the suitability of the media. The efficiency of any given channel is shown by the number of people the channel may reach multiplied by the propensity of the channel to reach the target audience. The effectiveness of the channel is driven by how well the specific channel will allow the brand to meet its goals.

Step 2: involves making judgements of suitability of the media to communicate the brand message. These channels are then scored against their ability to meet any key communications objectives. Workshops are run to capture historical experience, industry experience and any other relevant metrics. At the end of this process channels are categorised by their appropriateness, using a weighting approach.

Step 3: best time and place to use the media. The final process is called 'moments planning'. Using several qualitative techniques such as focus groups, depths, diary placements, ethnography, Naked gains insight into the product purchase cycle, the key consideration moments, and where and when communications will fall onto the most receptive ears.

COI – Sexually transmitted diseases – CASE STUDY

In the case of the Sex Lottery case study it was the times when thinking about unprotected sex was high on the agenda. Research (and common sense) showed these were social situations involving alcohol at pubs and nightclubs.

The Sex Lottery

Agency   Naked

Client   COI – Dept Health

Situation   Among 18–34 year olds the spread of Sexually Transmitted Infections is on the increase. Clinic visits have doubled over the last decade, driven mainly by more downmarket groups.

Objective	Public information campaign of sorts, delivering the key facts, challenging misconceptions and ultimately changing behaviour.
Insight	Linking the Lottery, a well-used and well-understood medium to the motivating proposition of 'The odds now of catching something from unprotected sex are shorter than you think'. Additionally, this simple, lottery-based language would appeal strongly to the key downmarket target audience and allow the delivery of 'new news' such as 'One person in nine has an STD.'
	In addition most unprotected sex happens under the influence of alcohol.
Campaign	The dual requirements of awareness and response prompted a two-tiered communications strategy, based on appropriate moments at which to affect such action:

Private Reception
Radio and press, being 'close' media consumed on a one-to-one basis delivered the core information in a personal way, allowing the message to 'hit home'.

Point of Shag (POS.)
Identifying moments when unsafe behaviour was on the agenda allowed the message to be placed where it would have the greatest potential for effect. Washroom posters, beermats and Sex Lottery scratchcards were distributed in pubs and bars, targeted for their more downmarket clientele and their proximity to key regional 'hot spot' areas.

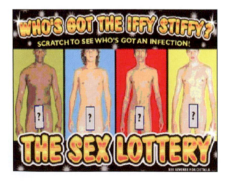 

Results	Detailed evaluation is underway. However, over 100,000 free condoms distributed in pubs and bars, with the venues also agreeing to allow the distribution of over 1.5m scratchcards free of charge.

THE COMMUNICATIONS CHALLENGE

Secondly, we review a tool called the Market Contact Audit MCA© from a company called Integration™, which is a specifically data-driven approach, involving both qualitative and quantitative research.

The MCA© is not intended to be a replacement for marketing intuition. Rather, it is designed to provide a framework to help guide intuition by creating a communications currency that allows the comparison and prioritisation of each and every contact that a brand has with its current and potential customers. Whilst it is not considered to be applicable to most B2B markets, the MCA© has been shown to work across a variety of consumer sectors ranging from FMCG to automotive, and from telecoms to banking.

It can help address some of the key questions facing marketers when addressing the increasingly fragmented communications landscape:

- What are the key contacts in my category and how do I prioritise them?
- Which contacts can help me to differentiate my brand?
- How is my brand performing in its communications versus my competitors?
- How can I better use contacts to optimise return on marketing investment and grow market share?

Approach: a category contact audit assesses 'contacts' for their:

- 'power' (a factor derived from consumer views about how 'informative' and 'attractive' that contact type is). This consumer perspective is gathered from initial qualitative and subsequent quantitative research.

- 'brand associations' (the extent to which that contact method is associated with that brand).

Example: Babycare Category Contact Audit

TV advertising	Brand mailings/newsletters
Press advertising	Brand website
Relevant press editorial	Family and friends
TV programme sponsorship	Instore displays
Recommendations by health and babycare professionals	Packaging
Free samples received at home	Instore promotion
Free samples received out of home (retail, leisure centres etc)	Instore demonstration
	Brand partnerships

The next step is, through analysis, to identify opportunities for a brand. The matrix locates channels according to how 'associated' they are with the market category (horizontal axis), and how 'potent' they are for the client brand (vertical axis). An example is shown below.

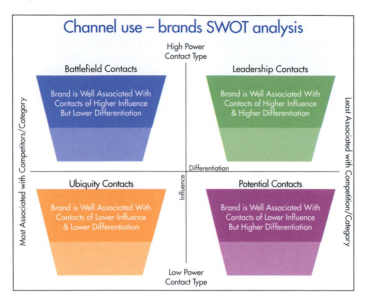

The model can then be used to guide future channel strategy, based on an understanding of how consumers perceive channels for their ability to influence their thinking, and to differentiate a brand in that category.

The MCA© is useful tool for media neutral planning and evaluation. It spans both channel planning and evaluation.

The common theme of both "Selecta" and "MCA©" however is that potential ways of contacting an audience are assessed and ranked by their ability to reach the communications objectives. Both approaches also include all types of communications media from TV, press and cinema, through the direct one-to-one and the hard-to-classify areas of PR and word-of-mouth.

Media neutral isn't necessarily multimedia

The IPA effectiveness awards show a trend towards multimedia campaigns. But this is not necessarily the outcome of the strategy processes described here. The gap analysis element of the MCA© tool could, for example, lead to a decision to concentrate on a particular medium for a variety of reasons – it's not one the competition use well, it's particularly well targeted, it's particularly good for conveying the message, competitive clutter, and so on.

Yellow – CASE STUDY

The next case study shows this. Research had shown that in the target market, use of public transport was key. Using this insight the agency worked with London Underground to create hundreds of new places to deliver messages about Yellow, culminating in the rebranding of a whole Tube train! The campaign created unprecedented levels of awareness and a substantial sales uplift for Yellow.

Yellow Pages/London Underground

Agency	PHD
Client	Yellow
Situation	Usage in London declining, especially in the Young age groups with increasing competitive clutter.
Objective	Yellow Pages needed to stem the decline in usage particularly among young socially active and reasonably affluent Londoners. Additionally, it wanted to encourage use of the directory and to be seen to do so by advertisers. Force the target market to reappraise Yellow Pages by communicating relevance to their lives in a dynamic and constantly surprising way.
Insight	Target market consumers are out a lot and use public transport heavily.
Actions	Outdoor was key and especially transport-related. The aim was to take the message to the target group as they went about their daily lives. PHD worked with London Transport to create new places to advertise from the back of tickets to departure boards, over 100

different creative executions were produced with the central theme of "painting the town yellow". The campaign famously rebranded a Circle Line (yellow) train.

Results   Yellow reported considerable revenue uplifts on the back of the campaign and Millward Brown tracking studies showed very high spontaneous awareness: Posters 80%, Buses 100% + Underground 300%. The campaign also won a Media award for best use of integrated media.

Partnerships between media and brands

Oliver Cleaver, European Media Director of Kimberly-Clark, has said *'Consumers have stronger relationships with media than they do with brands. The key is to harness that relationship to the brand.'*

More than this, in an increasingly cluttered media marketplace people often look to a few key media brands – which we described as editor brands in the introduction – as life guides or portals that select on their behalf. So, a matchmaking tool can be valuable. Media DNA looks at media brand values and thus enables planners to find a good fit and potential partnership with brands in general.

MediaDNA was created by Millward Brown and a group of six sponsors – British Sky Broadcasting, Capital Radio, IPC Media, News International and Yahoo! UK & Ireland and ZenithOptimedia. It is a survey of the views of over 5,000 UK adults about the country's leading 170 media brands, including national newspapers, major consumer magazines, principal radio stations and groups, and the main television stations. Together, these account for 80% of the UK's advertising spend in broadcast and national print media. The research examines the perceived personalities of a range of brands covering the five main media platforms: TV, radio, magazines, newspapers and the internet.

The study maps the media brands into three distinct areas: Image, Positioning, Personality. This allows advertisers to compare their products against 50 separate criteria to assess whether they are, for example, extrovert, glamorous, British or intellectual. The characteristics of each media brand can then be graphically plotted and compared to other brands. The new research tool also provides a metric to compare brands directly, irrespective of their media platform. The profile criteria for Image include Innovative, Family Oriented, British and Bold. The profile criteria for personality include, Playful, Intimate, Fussy and Rash. More information can be found at www.mediadna.co.uk.

Stella Artois – CASE STUDY

Sponsorship works best when there is a very strong fit between the media brand and the client brand. In this example, the agency used a key insight into a link between premium larger and film to initiate a sponsorship with Film 4, which has subsequently grown into more than 50 types of contact such as editorial content, events and cinema, including exclusive access to pre-released films.

Stella Artois
– Creating a point of difference with sponsorship

Agency   Starcom Motive

Client   Stella Artois – premium lager

Situation   In a crowded market with increasing pressure on price and small budgets Stella Artois had to find a way to reposition the brand.

Objective   The long-term marketing objective is to help make Stella Artois the No.1 beer brand.

Insight   Research showed that users of the product saw it as a premium product and something to be enjoyed/savoured rather than just guzzled. Additionally, film was disproportionately important to 18–34 premium lager drinkers in their leisure time. At that time Channel 4 was looking to increase the profile and credibility in the area of film.

Campaign   From modest beginnings in 1996, when film links were used to place ads, the relationship between Channel 4 and Stella has progressed and is central to the marketing of the brand with all media, PR, TV, Cinema, special magazines reflecting the relationship.

Results   Stella's association with film through sponsorship has had a disproportionate effect on spontaneous awareness. It shows the highest level of growth in drinkers and volume over the last 5 years indexing at 200 (penetration) and 375 (volume) in a market that is static and experiencing a loss of drinkers to FABs, vodka and spirit mixers.

Source: TGI/PAS/Alcovision

Optimising communication plans – Art and Science

There are a number of highly quantitative approaches to this. With sufficient data these models can be powerful predictors of performance. In contrast, some approaches involve the use of qualitative groups and subjective judgement. MediaCom Direct uses an 8-step approach outlined below:

Step 1:   Agree a target cost per customer at which it is profitable to acquire the customer or a return on investment (ROI) objective.

Step 2:   Agree the selection of media to be tested. This process should include:
* Review of all historical results.
* Regional implications.
* Seasonal implications.
* The index of efficiency of each title/station against key target groups.
* The cost of reaching a thousand viewers or circulation for each media type (CPT).
* The forecast response and conversion rate for each medium.
* The size of the test and rollout budgets (if the budgets are spread too thinly the results may not be statistically significant).

Step 3:   Test each media opportunity against the target cost per customer/ROI objective.

Step 4:   Establish a cost-efficiency ranking of each medium.
This chart simply shows example media costings with the response rates required to achieve a target cost per response of £10. The actual response and conversion rates are added after mature data from the tests become available. In practice, for example, direct mail will enjoy

Media	Size	Media CPT	Prdctn CPT	Total CPT	Response rate @ £10 CPR	Cost per response	Example Conversion rate	Cost per Customer
DRTV	30"	£3.00	Variable	£3.00	0.030%	£10.00	12.5%	£80.00
National Press	25 x 4	£3.23	£0.10	£3.33	0.033%	£10.00	12.5%	£80.00
Internet	Banners	£18.00	£0.05	£18.05	0.180%	£10.00	12.5%	£80.00
Door to Door	A4 folded to A5	£13.00	£13.00	£26.00	0.260%	£10.00	12.5%	£80.00
Inserts	A4 folded to A5	£17.00	£13.00	£30.00	0.300%	£10.00	12.5%	£80.00
Royal Mail Door to Door	A4 folded to A5	£28.66	£13.00	£41.66	0.417%	£10.00	12.5%	£80.00
Third Party	A4 folded to A5	£32.00	£15.00	£47.00	0.470%	£10.00	12.5%	£80.00
Direct Mail	Mail Pack	£100.00	£400.00	£500.00	5.000%	£10.00	12.5%	£80.00

higher response and conversion rates due to factors such as superior targeting, personalisation and proposition matching.

Step 5:   Validate the campaign results, optimising within each medium (within TV for example the most effective mix of copy, length, station and day part).

Step 6:   Replan the budget into the most efficient media.

Step 7:   Work towards saturation within each media: typically, the client would want as many customers as possible if they can be recruited at the profitable level.

Step 8:   Continue to optimise the campaign and develop the planning away from cost per customer into longer lifetime value measurements to maximise budget cost-efficiencies.

Egg – CASE STUDY

Egg combined a best-practice approach to brand response and direct marketing in an integrated campaign. They took a media neutral approach to media selection, 'rewarding' media which performed best against dual objectives with greater budget share.

Egg – using DM principles to optimise spend

Agency	MediaCom
Client	Egg
Situation	By 2002 Egg had built a strong financial services brand based on its competitive savings and credit card products. However, the high level of brand awareness achieved through a television-led strategy was not generating the volume of short-term sales to meet Egg's ambitious growth targets.
Objective	The communications objectives were to build long-term brand saliency as a platform to support the sales of multiple financial products, whilst at the same time achieving short term sales targets for individual products; in short, to integrate Egg's brand and direct marketing strategies.
Insight	Egg needed an integrated brand and direct marketing solution.
Campaign	Media test matrices were devised using a number of different URLs and phone numbers in order to assess the relative cost-efficiency of different creative approaches and media routes to market.

Econometrics were used to assess the impact of longer-term television brand responsive advertising on immediate direct marketing driven sales.

Direct marketing principles were applied to both the creative and media strategies.

Further consumer segmentation work was carried out to match brand and product propositions to key market subgroups.

By means of a series of media tests, MediaCom was able to build a media hierarchy of efficiency for Egg resulting in budgets being deployed into the most cost-efficient media channels to meet immediate product sales targets.

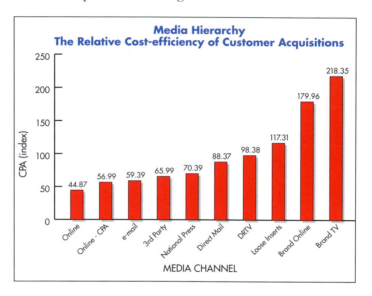

Media Hierarchy
The Relative Cost-efficiency of Customer Acquisitions

Results   This approach to high levels of accountability allowed Egg to assess the effect of brand activity on longer-term brand awareness and saliency, which in turn increased the propensity of prospects to respond and convert to the direct marketing activity. It also showed how the direct marketing activity could contribute to brand awareness and saliency target. The campaign reduced the overall cost per customer acquisition by 51%.

In contrast to highly quantitative approaches, NINAH, a marketing consultancy, uses a process it calls THOR™ which allows qualitative measures and judgement to be incorporated into the optimisation process. The approach has a quantitative side, however; here we are focusing on their use of a version of an approach called 'the Delphi technique' which was originally devised as a way of getting consensus views from a group of experts.

This qualitative approach can be useful as it starts to put values on factors that will clearly affect the performance of a campaign, but would be hard to build into a statistical model.

Such factors could be summer weather impacting ice cream sales, or a bad review from Jeremy Clarkson on a new car!

The technique also allows anonymous participation, which can be useful when there are political sensitivities over certain issues.

The Delphi Technique

The purpose of the Delphi technique is to elicit information and judgments from participants to facilitate problem-solving, planning, and decision-making. The technique uses questionnaires which can be emailed to participants. It also requires a Coordinator to organize the information, and to be responsible for communication with the participants.

Process

1. Identify the issue and solicit ideas. For example: what factors have an effect on our sales performance, and by what level?
Prepare and send the first questionnaire, which asks each participant to engage in individual brainstorming so as to generate as many ideas as possible for dealing with the issue.

2. Response to first questionnaire. Each participant lists his/her ideas (Questionnaire #1) in a brief, concise manner and returns the list anonymously to the Coordinator. No attempt should be made to evaluate or justify these ideas at this point in time.

3. Create and send Questionnaire #2. The Coordinator prepares and sends a second questionnaire to participants that contains all of the ideas sent in response to the first questionnaire and provides space for participants to refine each idea, to comment on each idea's strengths and weaknesses for addressing the issue, and to identify new ideas.

4. Response to second questionnaire. Participants anonymously record their responses to Questionnaire #2 and return them to the Coordinator.

5. Continuation of the process. If desired, the Coordinator performs iterations of the preceding process until it becomes clear that no new ideas are emerging and that all strengths, weakness, and opinions have been identified.

6. Resolution. Resolution may occur in one of two ways:
- If dominant, highly evaluated ideas emerge via consensus, the exercise is declared finished. The end product is a list of ideas with their concomitant strengths and weaknesses.
- The Coordinator conducts a formal assessment of the group's opinions of the merits of the ideas.

One method involves ranking the ideas, another voting for the top five.

Conclusion

Channel planning is truly where art and science meet. Channel proliferation and new technology have stimulated companies to get deeper knowledge of the properties and qualities of channels. This has been used to find more effective and innovative uses of media, both individually and in combinations.

The discipline of channel planning starts with clarity about expected outcomes from communications. There are several reasons for this. It provides:

- the criteria against which options can be judged.

- a springboard for creative and lateral thinking.

- the focus for a multidisciplinary team (all the case histories here required teamwork between media agencies, PR, DM and other communication specialists, creative agencies and the client).

Finally, clarity about outcomes means that evaluation methods can be designed, which is the theme of our next chapter.

Notes and References

(1) Alan Braithwaite 'The medium is part of the message – the role of media in shaping the image of the brand' *ESOMAR*, ed. Deborah Fellows

Chapter Five

Evaluation

Tony Regan and *Marie-Louise Neill*

Navigation box
The barriers to evaluation
Understanding aggregate effects
A framework for setting objectives
Measurement methods
Review of the tools of the trade
Disaggregating multichannel effects
Econometrics
Purpose-built models

Introduction

A neutral or unbiased approach to channel or media selection tends to lead to multimedia campaigns. Evaluation methods therefore have to deal with more complexity and it is vital that they do so to justify the investment of time and money. Individual media evaluation has advanced a great deal, multimedia campaign evaluation is a younger discipline and an important area of rigorous thinking and innovation. For the sake of simplicity this chapter will use the term 'channel neutral' to describe this discipline

This section is written in three parts. The first explains the precepts on which evaluation is, or should be, based. The second part provides an introduction to tools of the trade – how evaluation is carried out across a wide range of media. The last section illustrates how marketing communications professionals can go about synthesising media neutral evaluation from tools available today, plus some new, emerging, single-source evaluation approaches mainly being championed through media agencies.

The Barriers to Evaluation

For marketing and agency professionals whose work involves the exciting process of conceiving and implementing ideas, evaluation can seem difficult. However, evaluation is both the gateway to channel neutral planning, and potentially also the biggest obstacle standing in its way. So what are the barriers to doing it well?

1. *The desire to plan neutrally is often handicapped by the ongoing influence of established evaluation tools.* Hard-to-measure channels or media become less favoured while easy-to-measure channels, especially those that provide 'hard' rather than 'soft' measures, often have disproportionate appeal. New channels offering potential communications advantages to the marketer may be ignored because of problems in evaluation.

2. *It is intellectually challenging to be clear-thinking about your brand, defining what you want to know from evaluation.* Too little time is spent on defining objectives. Furthermore, evaluation involves specialist skills and approaches that can be daunting to non-specialists and these can frequently distract from identifying and sticking to the case in hand.

3. *It is almost impossible for an individual marketer to dismantle existing systems of evaluation.* Organisations are cautious about change. Even when all parties agree on the inappropriateness of some measures or even methodologies for the current times or tasks, it takes a brave company to let go of years of 'comparative' data and measure against real objectives.

4. *Evaluation is not the same as measurement.* Some of the most accountable activities could be 99% unsuccessful – but there's an appealing certainty about the 1% that does work. In assessing the performance of an ever more complex set of activities, there needs to be an acceptance that a cast-iron result is unlikely. There is no magic number that delivers an imperial thumbs-up (or not). There may not be a crystal-clear road map for next year. The web of effects created via interrelated communications can take a lot of untangling. There is a balance to be had between soft evidence and judgement in hard cash, between qualitative intuition and rigorous econometrics. Given that so much evaluation appears 'technical' and 'scientific', it's easy to get this wrong.

5. *There is a tendency to use evaluation as a post-mortem, or as a rear-view mirror.* Used this way it is inevitably unsatisfactory, leading to defensiveness, blame and evasion – particularly since multichannel activity depends on collaboration between agency teams. Not all communications work, and evaluation will help establish that, but there's no point in crying over spilt milk. Evaluation is about learning and what you do *next*, rather than what you did. Evaluation is the energising 'middle' learning period of a cycle between past activity and future activity, whether that's a timescale of weeks or calendar years. It sits at the beginning, in the middle and at the end of the communications planning process.

How did we get here?

Before dealing with the challenges of evaluation techniques, it helps to understand that the current range of evaluation tools reflects the way in which the media landscape has *evolved*. Just as different layers of sediment create different rock strata, each new channel has been laid down as a new layer of communications, each one inventing its own evaluation approach. And of course, the process is continuing, with new 'new' media emerging all the time.

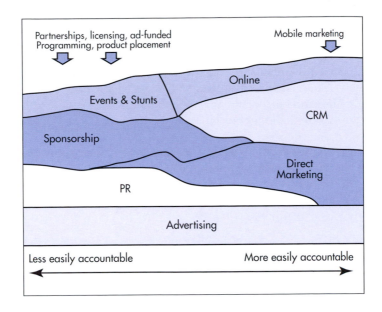

The proliferation of different, non-combinable or comparable evaluation techniques has made it hard for the marketer to evaluate activities, particularly with new channels where there are no established practices. Even in mature parts of the communications industry, those with long-standing evaluation practices and conventions, the real world is exhibiting rapid change, not least the fast-evolving relationships between consumers, brands and the media (in the broadest sense) which may throw the value of these techniques into question. This poses specific challenges for creating evaluation programmes appropriate for media neutral planning.

1. *Established evaluation measures have limited scope to evolve.* Traditional evaluation methodologies are each aligned with the channels they were built to serve. Consequently, most are relatively weak at detecting effects other than those anticipated by the communications model they derived from. Later, this chapter will show how existing evaluation methods can be adapted to broaden their usefulness, but the challenge remains that our collective thinking is often governed and constrained by the tools most easily available to us.

2. *There is a plethora of possible measures to choose from.* While established evaluation measures may have limitations, the variety of things that can now be measured generates a bewildering overload of information, and often raises questions about what to measure in the first place. From better sales data (from EPOS), to response analysis, online clicks, CRM database information, through to econometrics analysis informing budget allocation and channel choice, and calculations of advertising's contribution to brand value, it's clear that there are many things that *can* be measured. There's a need to decide where to invest effort, time and money, and then how to make sense of the information gathered, particularly when different categories of data are not immediately comparable.

3. *Short-term evaluation tools versus long-term evaluation tools.* It is a conundrum that while the industry has been getting more skilled at detecting and demonstrating *long-term* effects of communications, the fastest-growing channels (direct marketing and digital) currently only offer primarily *short-term* effectiveness and immediate measurability. All are valid and appropriate, but media neutral evaluation needs to bring together and balance the understanding of short- (and medium-) term activity with that of the longer term.

4. *The organisational dimension.* The relative credibility of information sources creates a working hierarchy of channel appeal. Some clients favour sales or response type measures, others tend towards brand image and reputation measures. Breaking down or questioning this hierarchy is necessary to create opportunities for fresh, objective planning.

5. *How much should be spent on evaluation?* What you spend on evaluation should be commensurate with the anticipated value from doing it. Bigger is only better if the enhanced data generated can be exploited cost-efficiently. It is tempting to believe that evaluation has to be quantitative, large-scale and specially commissioned, but there may be instances where

   - Smaller and qualitative approaches can be used to establish basic campaign registration, or to understand the effectiveness of a smaller experimental initiative.

   - Other sources of data serve just as well – e.g. behavioural measures including sales, response rates, web clicks etc. Here the task (and maybe a large part of the cost) is in making sure the data is accessible, useable and actionable.

The new sophistication in communications thinking

In response to channel proliferation, there has been a corresponding increase in understanding how channels can be used to implement communication programmes. A few of the key changes include:

1. *Our understanding of aggregate effects.* In the past, multichannel activity was limited for many brands, so it is only relatively recently that the effects of channel on channel have been recognised and studied.

   Typically, a neutral approach makes multichannel activity more likely, since the aim is to achieve 'multiplier' effects, i.e. more than simply the sum of the parts. We have visualised the way that channels combine to have their compound or aggregate effects simultaneously or sequentially, as two models – the 'Olympic' and the 'Domino' effect. In practice, most campaigns combine both.

   If the intelligent combination of activities provides multiplier effects, evaluation has to answer at least the following questions:

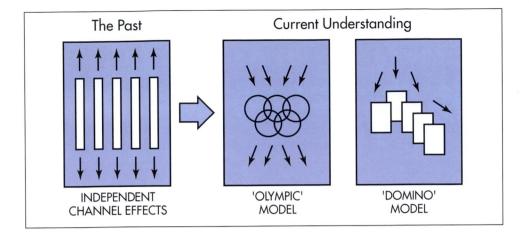

The Past	Current Understanding
INDEPENDENT CHANNEL EFFECTS	'OLYMPIC' MODEL / 'DOMINO' MODEL

- what did each channel deliver against its specific primary objectives?

- what did each channel deliver beyond its own specific primary objectives (e.g. DM enhancing brand health)?

- how did each channel enhance the performance of other channels in performing their roles?

- what was the combined effect on key communications activity measures (even if we can't attribute contributions to channels)?

2. *The 'multiskilling' of channels.* Increasingly, channels are used to perform roles that didn't historically 'belong' to them, e.g. using DM to build affection for and disposition to purchase a brand. In this case, as well as monitoring DM effects on behaviour, particularly response and sales, a brand-tracking methodology may need to be sensitive to the effects of DM activity.

3. *More roles for communication.* Not only are there more channels from which to choose for the same set of tasks, but communications perform *more* roles than before, as organisations seek different ways to do business with consumers. 'Opening dialogue', 'providing an experience', 'inviting interaction' – these are some of the new roles being performed.

> ### Expanding Roles for Communication *(not an exhaustive list)*
>
> - Communicate a brand's image or values (perceived emotional closeness).
> - Change a brand's image.
> - Launch a new brand.
> - Switch brands (convert users).
> - Sell product.
> - Retain loyal users.
> - Remind to use the brand (especially repertoire users).

- Extend consumers use of product – e.g. use product in a new time or season.
- Extend consumers use of product – e.g. new social or functional occasion.
- Try a new variant.
- Provide news/information/education to build brand use or loyalty.
- Maintain brand sales and defend from competitors.
- Justify a premium price position.
- Demonstrate product use.
- Help consumers differentiate advertised brand from others.
- Announce promotion.

4. *Multiple goals for communication.* With the multidimensional nature of brands, there's a growing requirement for a communications programme to achieve a *variety* of goals, among them:

- Reaching multiple audiences.
- Tangible brand effects (sales, footfall).
- Intangible brand effects (brand equity).
- Short-term and longer-term goals.

5. *Increasing emphasis on accountability & ROI.* A key task for a channel neutral approach is the objective assessment of channels for delivering *predictable* effects within a context of clearly articulated goals/expectations/benchmarks. This predictability is of major interest for clients focused on ROI, but a preoccupation with accountability tends to favour channels where effects are most easily measured, and often prioritises the identification of short-term effects, wherever they can be found.

Designing evaluation

A framework for setting objectives
Against the array of what a marketer can do, where is a marketer or its agencies to start? How do you decide which evaluation methods to use?

When a campaign is planned, whether in one medium for one audience, or for multiple channels and audiences, it helps to start by asking, 'What do you want to cause as a result of the activity?' The framework provided below starts from the premise that spending money on any marketing communications aims to make consumers either do something, hold an attitude, or perceive something about that brand which will affect future purchase behaviour.

Evaluation falls into two distinct areas:

- determining the degree to which overall marketing objectives are achieved; and

- determining the relative effectiveness of each channel in delivering the overall objectives. We can view this process as:

MARKETING OBJECTIVES	PLANNING ACTIVITY	EVALUATING THE RESPONSE
Setting objectives for desired consumer behaviour	Planning communications that affect consumer behaviour	Measuring a) Concrete consumer behaviour
(If I'm spending £1m on communications, how do I expect to see the performance of my brand and consumers' behaviour to change?)	Establishing i) Roles of communication ii) Measures for evaluation (a, b, c) iii) Measures for possible channel interactions/ unintended effects	b) Attitudes/perceptions towards the brand as a guide to future behaviour c) Registration of communications on consumers

Assessing the overall effectiveness of the programme against marketing objectives

Assessing the channel selection and media effectiveness

Evaluation requires a defined target, a specific time limit set for results, with a specific objective to achieve. Such objective-setting forces honesty between agency and client, and between a marketing client and their board-room colleagues. Several important consequences follow.

1. *You won't set measures that you don't need.* If success is defined as 'sales within 6 months', no amount of measuring emotional parameters relating to ad performance will help.

2. *You can plan a range of measures around brand effects.* If the plan is to get more people to try a brand, then measures leading up to and relating to trial can be developed.

3. *You can set measures appropriate to different target audiences.* What you measure for mums (sales, brand knowledge) may be different from what you measure with kids (attitude to brand, recall of ads, sponsorships, competition participation, web-visits etc). These may or may not be channel-specific. It is not uncommon for a brand to need to convey multiple messages. Whilst the objective of an advertising or direct marketing agency may be to identify one or two specific objectives, the role of PR is frequently to cover the field. Yet all these messages may go towards a consumer's final attitude or purchase intention.

Evaluation can examine consumers' behaviour, their attitudes to and perceptions of the brand, communication style, and whether they have truly 'received' communications intended for them. This framework provides a process for any marketer or agency to discuss objectives for the brand, objectives for communication and the evaluation measures that will demonstrate whether those objectives have been met. Some of these can be *observed* (behavioural measures), others are *reported* (attitudinal and reported behaviours).

Behavioural measures

'Do' measures are prized by marketers because they are generally observable and capable of objective measurement. You do more, do different, do at a different time, but there's always an observable behavioural difference.

Immediate changes to behaviour are often intended consequences of particular channel activity – sales promotion, direct marketing or new media, with immediate or short-term feedback on performance. Evaluation doesn't depend on asking consumers what they have done – the information can usually be gathered without asking.

Such measures include:

Doing Behaviours	Direct Measurement Possibilities
Purchase purchase a new variant purchase more purchase at a new time Use for a new purpose	Sales Incremental sales Sales over time Sales via new distribution channels
Trial – paid-for trials or reimbursable trials in particular	
Active enquiries about a brand or category/brand learning including: Brochure requests Web visits Phone calls Store visits	Consumers are mostly passive so when they make an effort to inform themselves we can measure actual uptake e.g. Brochure selection/ brochure request Website visit and visit duration, visit profile Phone calls to sales Footfall (shop visits)
Allowing permission to market to them – increasingly new channels fall into this category, e.g. Mobile marketing Permission-based CRM Loyalty cards	This is a more passive position on the part of the consumer but direct measurement of behaviours is still possible Mobile calls/offer uptake Sales Sales and incremental sales Member get member
Word of mouth. This can be positive or negative of course, but word of mouth recommendations are key for more brands than marcoms agencies generally admit	Member get member schemes

Participation in brand activities or community	Turn out to events Activity on, e.g. chat rooms and non-sales content within websites Care lines Product display by consumers (a memorable example being the display of Tango in bedroom windows)

Attitudes and reported behaviours

Apart from behavioural goals, you may desire measurement of the attitudes that occur before or alongside emergent behaviour. Gathering information about communications effects on attitudes or behaviour generally requires *asking* consumers, usually via quantitative survey.

Reported behaviour is what consumers say (or think) they have done. *Attitudes and perceptions* record what consumers claim to think and feel, and perhaps how they believe they will respond. These can be valuable measures *if* linked to actual behaviours. They can be diagnostic, providing comparison with competitive brands. They are popular because they can register subtle non-behavioural goals specific to particular messages.

Cognitive perception and *reported behaviours* include questions like:
- I always buy this brand.
- I have bought the product before.
- I am buying it more, recently.
- I have bought it for the first time.
- I would buy it again (repeat purchase).
- I would consider the brand in the future.
- I would never consider the product.
- I would consider it as my next purchase.
- Would be prepared to try a new variant.
- Would try this brand as a result of an offer.

Activities under consideration as a result of positive brand thoughts and feelings such as:
- Am aware that I can use the product in additional ways.
- Would recommend this brand to friends.
- This brand has the kind of ads that you talk about with friends.
- Worth finding out more about this brand.

Non-behavioural related thoughts and feelings that consumers report as part of brand awareness, image and equity studies e.g.
- I would rate this brand more highly than brand Z or specific 'batteries' of brand and product attributes to which consumers are supposed to have an attitude.
- Brand is active, feels like it's going places (momentum).

Source: Research International

Communication measures

Registration of communications provides an important opportunity to inform us about communications exposure. This can be sourced separately from syndicated media surveys, or reported/audited information about mailing volumes, or from other distribution methods for communications material. But it is usually better to supplement such data about *opportunity to see* with your own information gathered from proprietary research into *actual exposure* (most accurately determined by asking respondents if they recognise the material). The aim is to answer a number of relatively standard questions:

- Who has seen the communication (recognition and attribution)?

- Who has seen it versus who could/should have seen it (the media performance, when combined with sources such as BARB, NRS etc)?

- Where do they believe they have seen it (especially if you're trying to separate out 'matched luggage' communication programmes).

- What messages registered?

- Are these the intended take out of the communication? (Are there any unintended effects?)

- How intensely did these communications affect consumers? (This could be a question of impact or content.)

The aim often is to go beyond simple recognition and attribution towards diagnostics capable of helping the relevant agencies refine their understanding of the channel for next time.

The main issues to be wary of in reporting on what consumers think they have seen or heard are:

- the distorting effects of high brand awareness on claimed recall, with consequent misattribution to the brands.

- the over-attribution to TV versus other media in advertising.

- difficulty in recognition of non-TV communication – especially when a 'matched luggage' approach is chosen.

- measurability of some channels such as PR unless control 'samples' can be identified and measured.

- difficulty in identifying additional media effects such as sponsorship and disaggregation of such effects.

- the opportunity to miss negative effects. A good example of this is the danger of not recognising saturation effects on the consumer in terms of brand, rather than response rates. Our favourite example of this is a credit card issuer which bombards likely users with such frequency as to be positively irritating.

Tools of the trade

What are the key available tools used to assess total campaign effects and contributions made by complementary communications channels?

Key sources and tools include:

- Sales data, including, e.g. customer transactions, store traffic
- Response data (calls, coupons, clicks)
- CRM/Data about customer activity (from databases)
- Communication tracking studies
- Brand equity measurement
- Qualitative research, observation and filming
- Econometric modelling

Sales data

Analysis of sales data has advanced as a discipline in line with the improvement in data generated by EPOS, especially analysis conducted by retailers who have unmediated access to this data source. Sales data has also been a focus for ever-advancing statistical modelling techniques.

A key issue is ensuring that sales data is collected in a way that allows analysis of how communications stimulated those campaign effects. For example, if communications programmes vary by region, it's important to have sales, response and customer activity data that can be regionally segmented.

Some are happy to start and end evaluation here – a 'nothing else matters' approach. That may be fine if you are operating in a growing market, or one where sales are particularly sensitive to communications activity. However, for many brands in stable or declining markets, where the role for communications is to defend existing sales, a conclusion of 'no sales increase' would hardly be a true assessment of the communications' performance.

Response data

Direct marketing and direct response media planning are based on data-driven planning and evaluation so it is a prerequisite that the necessary data will be collected for assessing the performance of activity. Direct marketing focuses on interrogating this core response data to answer key questions and optimise future activity:[1]

- Response rate
- Volume of leads
- Cost per lead
- Lead quality with a good level of potential
- Lead to sale conversion rate
- Cost per sale
- Profitable customer acquisition

There is usually no shortage of 'data', but typical problems include imperfections in data quality (e.g. the media source attributed by the caller for a telephone response), or a collective obsession with one key performance indicator, blinding the project team to considering any other measure.

The key is to build systems that can use response data constructively. For example, when Esure began, it created a system that would use response data as the basis for a consistent planning process from segmentation through to targeting and implementing the communications process.

Esure: making response data the common currency for communications planning

Esure's actuaries identified a segment of 'safe' drivers, defined by age, car type, and attitudes to such things as driving, routine and safety.

Initial analysis at the communications planning stage identified the potential for geodemographic markers (from MOSAIC) to generate the segment definitions.

This provided a 'common currency' for planning across advertising and direct marketing media, as well as a benefit at the evaluation stage because every consumer responding could then be classified by postcode, providing immediate assessment of communications performance against geo-demographically-defined segments.

Source: Media Planning Group

Direct Marketing response data – principles

Direct Marketing uses response data to test communications effectiveness. The mantra is 'test, test, test', using test and control techniques which involve building statistically valid cell sizes for mailings that will allow accurate comparison of how each piece performs against another.

Given that response rates in DM now rarely exceed 2%, it's important to be certain whether a 1.4% response against a 1.5% response represents a real difference or not. The data analysts use complex formulae to calculate the smallest size a campaign can be in order to make meaningful judgement.

Variables can be tested quite easily – these include anything from targeting who is being mailed to creative (one pack versus another) to the offer (early bird incentive to respond versus no incentive). Even very small details about execution – such as the style of envelopes used – can be evaluated and can have a strong material effect on the ROI, forecast response rate, mailing size and frequency.

A good example in action is analysis carried out by Proximity for the TV Licensing Authority. Here, testing showed a clear difference in performance between a single window envelope (with the customer's name and address) compared with a double window envelope which showed name and address and a show-through that announced that TVL enforcement officers would be visiting that street shortly. The second envelope uplifted response (with no other changes at all) by 0.9%, which equated to £10,000 of revenue.

Direct response advertising, usually press, is normally evaluated by using split executions with separate phone numbers. Here, the typical problem for press and insert responses is that call handlers are often not good at recording where somebody saw an ad, and indeed consumers may not be that good at remembering. While media codes are a reasonable substitute, they are not particularly helpful if you end up with most response being attributed to an 'unknown' box – it's common for over half the responses to a campaign to end up being unattributable to a publication. To minimise the problem, direct marketers recommend using a different phone number for every piece.

There are three challenges for direct marketing evaluation:

1. Difficulty of pre-testing. One reason for the extensive post-implementation evaluation of content in DM is the difficulty of pre-testing. When you show DM in a qualitative research environment, consumers prefer pieces that look most like brand work and least like direct marketing. However, it's a well-quantified truth that the more it offers, and 'selling' a piece of DM is, the better it works. So, some agencies are beginning to develop quantitative pre-testing methodologies that give a more 'truthful' read.

2. Determining the impact of DM on customer's propensity to buy over time. Traditionally, agencies have treated the performance of a single piece of DM as independent of other DM, and determined its success through cost per acquisition or cost per response (other variables obviously exist), or ROI, or volume or value. What is less clear is what the effect is on the 98% of people who didn't respond, or indeed whether the 2% that did were influenced by previous mailings. This is less likely to be an issue for something such as mailings about loans, where the need is immediate or irrelevant, but can be a real issue for a new car launch, where a consideration/buying window can take over 12 months. For purchases with long consideration times, it may well be that cumulative impact matters. Today, only the final mailing – the one that customers responded to – would be deemed successful.

    The importance of this question cannot be ignored. For instance, a bank may mail you every month with a variety of messages; the simple act of them sending mailings makes customers feel engaged and valued as well as reminding them of services and keeping the brand at the top of their minds. The impact of these communications may be profound, even when there is no response. Increasingly, to evaluate sequences of communications not just single 'shots', conjoint analysis is being used, using the same process of test and control cells (some getting all the communications, others getting a proportion and some getting none). In a multistage programme, therefore, agencies are now able to measure programmes, knowing that the response will not come until all four pieces have worked their magic, but that stage 1 is (say) 30% responsible for the final sale.

3. Assessing brand impact of the channel. This is still relatively new territory, as brand-tracking studies typically don't work in the same way that a mailing programme is developed; or rather, objectives for a mailing programme do not specifically include a brand task. This is important because it is not until we can evaluate brand impact properly that CRM will fully demonstrate its worth. At the moment, there is usually too little evidence to say that building warm

relationships with existing customers over long periods of time delivers a serious return to the bottom line.

Online direct response

Until recently, 'click-throughs' were regarded as a seductively straightforward metric, widely adopted as representative of either direct responsiveness or of brand impact of online advertising. Practitioners now recognise that brand impact can be appropriately collected from online research with respondents who are identified at the point of exposure to the online advertising, while pure response can be measured by collecting data on people who actually proceed to a sale or an actual request for information. Using these metrics, or combining them, can provide marketers with real knowledge of the cost of advertising and website effectiveness.

CRM/Database marketing

As the sophistication of database management increases, CRM is becoming more important as a source of information about communications performance, and a critical support to the development of media neutral planning for three key reasons:

- Paid-for activities such as DM and advertising can be interrogated, customer for customer.
- Customers increasingly prefer to provide data about themselves as part of their relationship with an organisation, rather than by participating in sample-based survey research.
- Speed, currency of data and the cost of information for data supplied in this way may be better than survey approaches.

Organisations with highly developed customer management systems have detailed knowledge about the behaviour of their customers. The best example of this is in current account banking, where banks have knowledge of most of the customer's income and spending. The example below shows how First Direct built on that customer knowledge to create opportunities for more effective communications.

First Direct – using customer research surveys to add to database knowledge and develop more relevant communications

Instead of the conventional approach, where learning from research leads to marketing activity against *similar* customers to the ones in the sample, First Direct interviewed individual customers about their anticipated needs from financial products and services and then applied the information they gathered (with customers' permission) to each person's file on the customer database. This then drove communications strategy so that, for example, mailings on credit cards or savings accounts were only sent out to customers who had said they might be interested in them. This 'permission marketing' initiative has enhanced marketing performance. Knowledge of customers' response rates can be set against actual sales conversion, and against the cost of activities to achieve an overall sales efficiency.

Source: First Direct

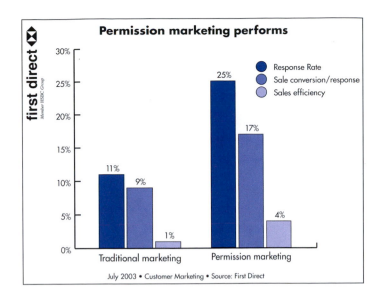

Permission marketing performs

first direct
Member HSBC Group

- Response Rate
- Sale conversion/response
- Sales efficiency

Traditional marketing: 11%, 9%, 1%
Permission marketing: 25%, 17%, 4%

July 2003 • Customer Marketing • Source: First Direct

Communication tracking studies

In the past, tracking studies have been used primarily to identify the registration and impact of advertising on brand perceptions. To do that properly, a 'continuous' approach became best practice, i.e. interviewing weekly or monthly throughout the year rather than simply around a period of communications activity. Tracking studies provide:

- diagnostic information on content.
- the opportunity to assess competitors' communication activities as well.
- opportunity to check media consumption/ channel habits.
- a high data quality fit for econometric analysis of brand effects.

Best practice is that, wherever possible, actual recognition (rather than recall) of communications material should be used. Increasingly, this means research execution using web, CAPI or PDA-based research methodologies, which allow for high-quality visuals, sound and video to be shown to consumers.

Some things to be aware of when creating trackers of any kind:

- Whenever you have to ask consumers what they think they have done, there will be over- or under-reporting, depending on the type of behaviour, its social acceptability, its importance to consumers and its frequency, and indeed whether it is top of mind or not. The simplest demonstration of this principle is the over-reporting of sex by men when compared with women.

- Asking consumers what they think may lead to a higher level of thought than they have ever given the category before. This provides marketers with the mistaken belief that consumers ARE interested in elements that in practice barely register, for example, functional attributes that the consumer usually gives little thought to.

- When consumers are asked what they think, unless the issue is a sensitive one, they rarely have a reason to lie, but may want to please. Evidence is emerging that e-surveys produce more honest, if less positive, answers than face-to-face or telephone interviewing. Data quality and in particular, utility of verbatims, is often much higher.

- No claims about behaviour can be taken in isolation of availability and price – but these can be easily overlooked when compiling the questionnaire.

- If you are building a custom tracker, there's a tendency to 'boil the ocean' – covering more issues than are strictly necessary, or borrowing measures off standard trackers which have little relevance to the questions you need to ask and answer.

- Sample selection can be critical – see boosts below.

Whilst continuous tracking is essential if you are determined to unpick events in a multimedia communications plan, for many other communication programmes much cheaper regular 'dipsticks' can suffice.

Alternatively, to avoid losing the benefits of continuous data, much leaner continuous trackers can be devised. This means interrogating the goals of your communication, and really focusing the scope of the research. They do give answers to the specific questions you have asked, and can be cheap and efficient.

Adapting trackers to the requirements of a neutral approach
A major challenge for traditional tracking methodologies, however, is giving a 'fair hearing' to different channels, or types of media. Often, the ambition to adapt is to avoid the cost of setting up tracking in each category. A cost-effective solution might regularly tag 'boosts' to create a 'fishbone' tracking approach, as illustrated below.

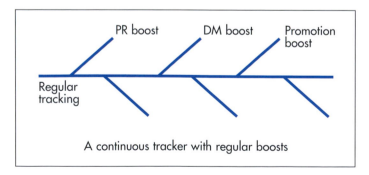

A continuous tracker with regular boosts

Such customisation can be suitable where a brand has a dominant medium, or where the main role is to assess whether the communications are working, rather than how well they are working, against a target audience. If very detailed channel by channel knowledge is required, mere adjustment of an existing advertising tracker is unlikely to satisfy long term.

A reason for boosts is to capture responses from minority media or audiences. For example:

- if you want to target those who regularly read a magazine, so that these readers can be compared to non-readers of the magazine in the overall channel mix.

- if, say, your outdoor activity has high 'reach', but your press and radio activity doesn't, you may not be able to pick this up in a standard sample, and so may require boosting the sample of those who listen to radio/read press.

In assessing one-to-one activities, sampling non-respondents and rejectors provides a good comparison against those who did respond. Equally, the use of matched samples can provide a control to measure incremental effects from secondary media, or from complementary channels such as sponsorship or PR. A good example of this comes from Emap Advertising, who develop cross-media advertising packages for clients, exploiting the full breadth of Emap's media properties in magazines, radio, TV and online. Typically, these packages involve editorial and promotions as well as advertising space and airtime.

This example shows the evaluation of some activity developed for Foster's, who sponsor Formula 1 and wanted to leverage more value from that by communicating the fact to FHM readers in a motivating way. Emap developed an integrated campaign built around the FHM brand and supported by other parts of their portfolio.

Foster's F1 Pit Girls

Online FHM.com	Advertorial content Accreditation icon on Girls Home Page Fosters co-branded solus emails (viral mechanic contained) Editorial slots on FHM weekly newsletter Incorporation into FHM.com editorial Editorial publicity boxes Incorporated into navigational bar Banners within FHM.com Banners run on Emap network
Magazines FHM magazine	DPS Advertorials Advertorial content driver/competition
Emap magazines	Joint branded ads
Radio Big City Network	Winning weekend promotion Breakfast show promotion
Kiss 100 FM	Breakfast show promotion Winning weekend promotion
Television Emap TV	QTV, Kerrang, Kiss 10" idents Kiss TV Voting Promotion

The challenge for evaluation was in distinguishing the contribution made by different parts of the mix. This was achieved by structuring the post-campaign quantitative research sample carefully around people's exposure to different combinations of the activity, including a control group who had no exposure.

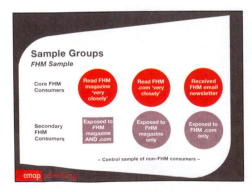

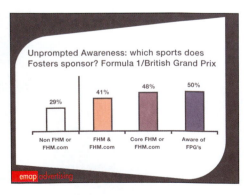

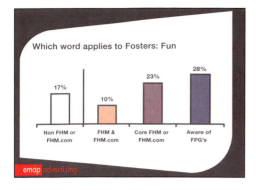

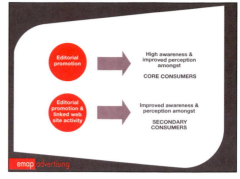

Among the findings were that the online activity had been particularly effective in driving communications amongst 'secondary' FHM consumers.

Another example is the launch of Boots No7 Intelligent Colour Foundation, where the impact of a mailing to Advantage cardholders was derived from a tracking study tailored to be sensitive to non-TV effects.

Boots No7 Intelligent Colour Foundation

Background
A new cross-disciplinary client team (brand, consumer insight, DM (Advantage Card), PR and communication channel planning) focused on media neutral planning. Team established in time to plan launch of No7's Intelligent Colour Foundation product.

The product
Boots No7 Intelligent Colour Foundation a revolutionary product that adjusts to the colour of the user's skin for a soft and natural effect. Consumers simply choose between light/medium/dark variants of the product. The launch provided an opportunity to support sales of the product as well as driving positive perceptions of Boots and No7 (the second biggest colour cosmetics brand in the market).

Channel planning
Advertising activity for Boots No7 typically planned into TV and women's magazines. In addition, the team further recommended PR to support a revolutionary and exciting new product, and mailings to the Advantage cardholder base.

- Cardholders are frequent and/or loyal shoppers at Boots, typically with positive perceptions towards the main brand and to Boots No7.

- Opportunity to identify previous purchasers of cosmetics and of Boots No7.

Role for evaluation
- Assess the performance of this initial activity.

- Provide evidence to support the aims and achievements of the new media-neutral team.

- Provide data for future media neutral planning.

- Overcome the limitations of previous tracking research which the team believed lacked sensitivity for detecting any non-TV effects.

Evaluation activity
- Store-based model introduced to detect sales on a store-by-store basis (e.g. with/without TV, with/without mail, with/without store promotions).

- Enhanced tracking study:
  a. media exposure attribution derived from viewing/reading questions rather than claimed ad awareness
  b. matched samples for mailed/non-mailed respondents

Tracking study results
Clear evidence that mailing programme performed extremely well:
- higher awareness of new product amongst mailed (three quarters) than non-mailed (less than half).

- more than half of mailed respondents (spontaneously), and two-thirds (prompted), claimed they first heard about the brand from a 'leaflet through the post'.

- product proposition understood by twice as many mailed respondents (vs non-mailed).

- higher levels of 'intention to try' amongst mailed respondents (more than half) compared with non-mailed (a third).

Calculations demonstrated that mailings generated awareness points at 64% of the cost of more TV for reaching the same consumers.

PR Tracking Systems

So much has been written about proprietary advertising tracking systems, that there is little need to write more. However, methods for using tracking to assess PR, which can be a big part of a brand's communication, are less well known and even less well practised. PR often suffers from the notion, widely subscribed to, that it is 'impossible to evaluate'. This is not true.

A basic approach to evaluating PR is to calculate the gross impressions delivered through the media, and to assign a monetary value from media owner ratecards for equivalent advertising space or time. An enhanced version of this technique, also widely used, is to attach a factor (typically 'favourability') so that not only the amount of coverage is considered, but also its potential to contribute to brand health. The Institute of Public Relations (IPR) has produced guidelines for media evaluation that sets out the process for analysing coverage.[2]

However useful these measures are, they only help us understand the *media* aspects of PR (PR can comprise, and often does, a much broader range of activities), and as such can only evaluate 'output'. More sophisticated tracking can establish the contribution of PR – where 'PR' encompasses a wider range of activities – in achieving 'outcomes'.

Here is an example of one such PR tracking tool.

The i to i tracker® measurement system

This methodology is used to assess PR either working together with other channels to create a compound effect, or showing how hard PR (or other channels) is working to deliver a solus effect.

It combines secondary sources with a survey-based approach, and uses a common sequence of analysis derived from advertising tracking (reach, awareness, communication takeout and preference/purchase intention). The approach uses a common framework across all channels for assessing their performance in delivering:

- penetration.
- proposition (message out-take).
- preference.
- prompting action.

It tackles recall of communications activity in different channels via carefully-worded questions and via analysis comparing the ad-exposed against the PR-exposed, in conjunction with further analysis of media-reported exposure (e.g. BARB or NRS).

i to i tracker is a registered trademark of i to i tracker Limited, a wholly owned company in the Publicis Group

---

Brand equity measurement

Brand equity measurement is one of the fastest-growing techniques for marketers. It can be conducted on a continuous basis, or in dips, monthly or six-monthly. Unlike econometric analysis, or a typical communications tracker, it makes no attempt at disaggregating channel effects – that is not its purpose. It is there to decide if the content of your communications and overall mix is achieving the brand goals you set.

Brand equity measurement per se does not need to be 'soft'. It comes in a variety of forms, a few being linked to accounting models based on the goodwill estimate for a brand (i.e. the premium over hard assets) that a brand is estimated to be worth. But the dominant trend for brand equity measures and models has been to provide a diagnostic approach to the effect of *message content* on brands over time; for example, the consumer's estimation of a brand's functional benefits, emotional benefits and price.

The best way to think of such an equity measurement model is to provide the marketers with a 'rudder' for steering messaging within the brand's 'content' objectives. If, for example, you need more of a particular emotional dimension, your brand equity tracker should, over time, tell you if you're getting it, and you may, as such models grow in sophistication, be able to work back to the channel to establish the channel's impact on this brand dimension. But like a rudder, it will not be instant; such measures move slowly.

Brand equity trackers can provide measures of brand *momentum*. This useful concept estimates a brand's activity level in consumers' eyes, rather like nautical speed (to continue the sailing boat analogy). How fast the boat is going determines which boat consumers want to be on. The principle is that consumers are more drawn to a brand that they perceive as being adopted and endorsed by others. This may be stimulated or conveyed by communications activity.

Importantly, brand equity measures should be viewed as independent of communication measures. Whilst it is possible to see the effect of communication on brand equity, brand equity shifts are not solely dependent upon communications.These may be caused by other activities.

However, measuring brand equity components can:

- give an early-warning system to marketers (useful for planning next year's activity) by establishing content needs from communications, usually in response to the loyalty or switching potential of consumers to the brand;

- help refine the balance of communications. For example, a marketer can experiment with whether brand momentum goes up if certain activities are increased amongst a specific audience;

- provide input on positioning and comparison to competitors, without the expense of following all the twists and turns of a competitor's campaign. Answering the question 'better than brand x' is not an idle question. The answer to the question 'How fast do you have to run to out run a black bear?' is 'faster than the other guy'. And so it is in marketing.

Qualitative research, observation and filming

Qualitative research can provide quick, relatively inexpensive and target-specific feedback on which communications are salient, convincing and effective. The disadvantages are obvious if the requirement is statistical robustness, but these approaches can be very useful and convincing as support or reassurance to the decision-making team.

Qualitative research need not be limited to a few focus groups. Exit-interviews from shops, cinemas and leisure venues, or on-street vox pops are also useful. Observation, often referred to as ethnography nowadays, is also well-suited to getting feedback on the net effect of multiple communications, rather than unpicking the contributory effects of each channel. For instance, are children picking up playground games around a brand? Or do people adopt phrases or mannerisms from packaging and advertising?

Observation including filming is commonly used in retail marketing to monitor consumer behaviour. Used in conjunction with other behavioural information (like sales) or data from interview-based research, it can provide conclusions about how communications affect behaviour. It has the advantage of being relatively low-cost and convincing early feedback, ideal for highly targeted activities such as field marketing, demonstrations, displays, point of purchase activity, instore promotions.

Econometrics

Econometrics is a statistically-based approach, which cross-relates or models data you gather to determine effectiveness of activities and assigns a financial result, thereby calculating the return on investment. Its strength is that it can combine several data sources. It is a cornerstone of many IPA Effectiveness papers, and is now offered to clients almost universally by the biggest media agencies. Successful econometrics demands the following:

- high-quality time-series data

- initial investment (although it typically generates information that creates budget savings bigger than the cost of analysis)

In addition, it's a tool for explaining *historic* events – there are no guarantees that circumstances will be the same for future planning.

Finally, the sophistication of the approach can sometimes disguise the uncomfortable reality of inadequate data quality, leading to interpretational difficulties; more simply described as 'rubbish in-rubbish out'. Assessing the data involves:

- Counting everything in terms of weekly impact on consumers and the cost of doing it.

- Doing lots of things, at lots of different levels (high, medium, low), not always at the same time as other things, so you can disaggregate effects later.

- Factoring in effects e.g. competitive action, economic and external factors, then analyse to achieve ROI per channel, or per customer per channel.

Econometrics therefore is very useful for disentangling the effects of *multichannel* communications.

Attributing campaign effects to channels

Many organisations will be satisfied to assess aggregate effects. However, in this final section we provide a number of examples of how campaign effects have been *disaggregated* where two or more channels have been used. This is putting together methodologies – most commonly enhanced survey-based approaches (tracking), and econometric modelling. It also highlights some new purpose-built approaches to gathering information for media neutral planning and evaluation.

Disaggregating PR, Sponsorship and Advertising
It's useful to see how tracking approaches can be used to assesss the solus and complementary effects of PR, advertising and sponsorship. The following examples illustrate how this is done.

Evaluating PR and advertising for Microsoft X-Box at Christmas
Microsoft's strategy in the run-up to its first Christmas season after the launch of X-Box was to use advertising and PR to push sales of specific X-Box games titles around the campaign theme 'Play More'.

Key communications objectives were:

- build reach and frequency through the combination of ads and PR.
- communicate the 'Play More' message.
- engender preference towards the X-Box brand.
- create demand for X-Box consoles.

The activity was evaluated using carefully worded questions to accurately get at claimed recall of activity in different channels, and via analysis comparing the ad-exposed against the PR-exposed.

Analysis provided a clearer understanding of what PR had achieved *solus*:

- significant media reach and frequency, leading to strong levels of recall.
- higher awareness of Play More slogan than ad-only sample.
- greater brand preference and interest in buying X-Box.

... and what it had achieved jointly with advertising:

- gamers exposed to both advertising and PR were 50% more likely to recall 'Play More' slogan.
- higher brand preference and purchase consideration scores amongst PR/ad aware group.

Source: i to i tracker

In the following example, a 'Domino' model of advertising and PR resulted in the following evaluation application. This section shows how the impact of sponsorship of a sports event could be identified, using the technique of adding boosts to a long running tracking study.

Evaluating the Contribution of Sponsorship to C&G
Cheltenham & Gloucester (C&G), a major player in the very crowded market providing mortgages, savings and investments, knew that a strong positive relationship existed in this marketplace between brand salience (as measured by spontaneous *brand* awareness) and consideration to use a financial supplier.

Historically, the main driver of brand salience had been television advertising. When the decision was taken to add cricket sponsorship, HPI, the research company responsible for its existing tracker, was asked to provide a basis for evaluation of this activity that could be directly comparable with TV experience. The methodology involved "twinning" the regular tracker with an additional sample of men who followed cricket. The cricket-following samples fed back direct responses to C&G's involvement with the game:

- 42% association with the activity in 2001, rising to 56% in 2002
- just under 90% endorsed the appropriateness of fit between sponsor and sport

For the key comparative brand salience evaluation the data source was the regular tracker. A pitfall to avoid was autocorrelation – because people most familiar with a brand are automatically more aware of *all* marketing activity.

As a result, the researcher, HPI, compared spontaneous brand awareness for the total sample with that for those who neither followed cricket nor had had contact with the limited C&G tournament-supporting press campaign in the sports pages of specific newspapers. In other respects – notably ownership of any C&G account – the samples were identically matched.

The result for both years was a consistent brand salience advantage that could be compared directly with the lift generated by TV activity.

Cricket Sponsorship Brand Salience Lift		*TV Generated Brand Salience Lift*	
2001	+3%	Average for last 4 bursts	
2002	+4%		+6%

The final element of this media neutral evaluation was to relate these results to the costs involved and thereby to directly compare the efficiency of the two marketing activities on a common basis known to relate to business generation.

Source: HPI

Disaggregating advertising and DM

Disaggregating advertising from DM is a frequent need. In this case, adapting a tracking study provided a way to assess combined effects. Here, the essential ingredient was to give each medium an equal opportunity in its own environment. For example, it would not be fair to use a standard 'brand and advertising' approach to assess a national TV campaign running alongside a door-to-door leaflet drop in specified postcodes or direct mail addressed to individuals from a database. And apparently media neutral awareness questions, where each medium is listed separately, will not be media neutral if some of those media only aim to achieve, say, 5% coverage on a national basis.

Tracking advertising and DM in combination for Brand A

For Brand A, the solution for isolating the contribution of direct marketing as part of a multimedia campaign was to set up a test control study where a test sample of consumers was additionally exposed to direct mail. The reason for this approach was that a nationally based, representative sample would have been too broad and insensitive to measure the effect.

The findings demonstrated the power of direct mail, and its potential role in future multimedia campaigns, as illustrated below.

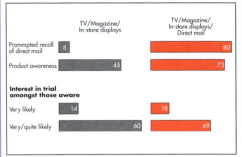

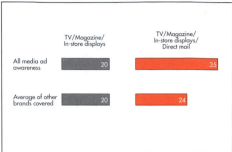

Source: Researchcraft

Statistical modelling comes into its own when faced with the challenge of integrated brand and direct response campaigns. While the statistics in the approach are complex, the technique seeks to answer some fairly easy-to-ask questions. Simon Foster, of PHD Confidential, highlights typical enquiries:

- Does running above the line awareness activity affect lead volumes in direct response media?

- Do conversion rates fall if mainstream awareness activity stimulates too many leads?

- Is the overall cost per lead greater or lower when run in conjunction with other forms of activity?

- Does awareness generation activity increase the speed of the sales conversion process?

- Are leads gathered when integrated activity is running more valuable than those obtained when single media campaigns are running?

- Are spend levels higher from consumers recruited while awareness activity is running?

- Are customers acquired from any one medium more or less loyal than those from another?

To illustrate the clarity that can be obtained, the following table from First Direct's IPA Effectiveness paper shows how econometrics was used to calculate the enhancement effect of TV advertising on the performance of direct marketing and direct response press activity:

Such evidence helps marketers make better decisions about how channels work together, rather than just deciding 'which channel works best'.

Chapter Four featured a case history concerning Egg, showing how a common assessment method assessment for all DM and brand activity enhanced the planning process by identifying a hierarchy of media and channels to inform budget allocation. At the end of the process, econometrics was the tool that allowed the agency to model the enhancement effect of advertising on DM and vice versa. The econometrics activity identified key relationships:

- the impact of brand awareness/saliency on consumers' propensity to respond/convert to DM activity.

- DM activity's contribution to brand awareness and saliency.

Disaggregating multiple channels

The following example shows how a retailer disaggregated the store experience from other media, and illustrates the importance of time-based assessments. This reflects reality for many marketers, faced with a huge range of long and short term communication activities, plus a range of response data, sales data and tracking information to hand. Here, the retailer used econometrics to assess performance.

Understanding the contribution of multiple communications for a UK grocery retailer

A UK grocery retailer with an extensive communications programme was debating the effectiveness and contribution of TV advertising compared to more tactical approaches. As part of its strategy to bring consumers in, it had loyalty schemes and used door to door and product promotions extensively. Another question was the role of 'refits' – did these really draw in consumers or not? Like most retail businesses, frequency of store visit is key, so understanding the effect of more corporate image elements such as the refits and advertising was a priority.

After an econometric analysis, the retailer was able to draw up both short- and medium-term implications. Looking at the results, the retailer concluded that brand TV, the results of which were less obvious in the short term, did have a role to play in the longer term. This helped the marketing team to be more confident about traditional brand advertising. The retailer was also able to contextualise the refit programme, which was slowed, focusing on urgent cases only. Money was moved into leaflets, PR and TV. With no change in the marketing budget, sales revenues increased by 7% year on year.

Sales & Marketing strand	Short term revenue ROI (one month)	Medium term revenue ROI (one year)
Brand TV	5:1	16:1
Product/Promotion TV	4:1	8:1
Leaflets Door to door	7:1	7:1
Brand PR	4:1	6:1
New loyalty scheme	6:1	5:1
New stores		5:1
Old Loyalty scheme	4:1	4:1
Sports Sponsorship	4:1	4:1
Store refits		3:1
Regional press	3:1	2:1
National press	2:1	2:1

Source: Manning Gottlieb ROI Metrics

It should be remembered that econometric analysis can isolate the advertising channel from external economic factors and other marketing effects such as price, distribution and competitive activity. In the following example, we illustrate how important this can be.

Understanding the economic and competitive landscape in the case of a UK health brand.
The first step for this UK health brand was to make sense of its marketing communications spend, divided into specific marketing programmes, ranging from general brand communication to specific tactical activities including product/price promotions, seasonal programmes.

These are shown below, and illustrate how TV advertising contributed to sales of a given product within the brand.

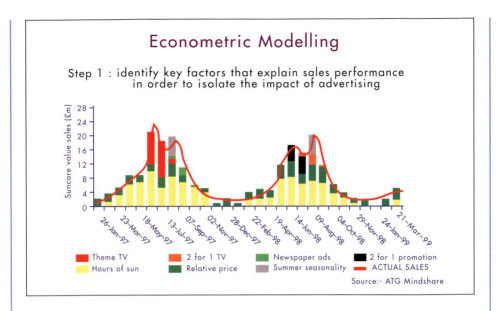

The second step for the brand was optimise its media spending.

This was achieved by drawing up the sales/response curve. By doing this, the marketing team could understand at what level of expenditure or weight this medium became less effective due to diminishing returns, as the chart below illustrates.

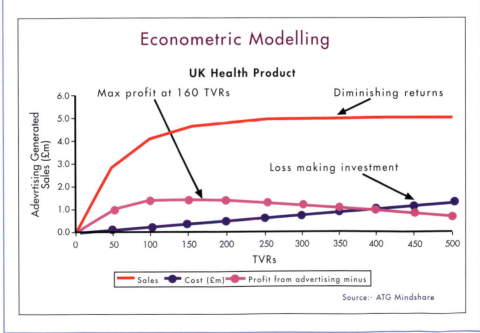

Purpose-built multichannel evaluation

The examples we've seen so far show best practice in linking together the learning from multiple data sources, or in adapting an existing evaluation tool (tracking, or response analysis) to a dual channel or multichannel situation.

In an effort to develop a better approach, some agencies have been working on purpose-built studies that enable key metrics to be more accurately assessed using data from a single survey. They all recognise the reality that consumers have many touch-points with brands, and all attempt to provide guidance about how to identify the most powerful channels and to manage budgets across them.

MCA (Market Contact Audit), which has been detailed in the previous chapter as a channel planning tool, is also used for campaign evaluation. Another method, in this case developed and implemented over the past three years by media agency Carat, is a system known as Cognitive Tracking. It measures the contribution of each and every contact point to the consumer experience of the brands audited. It uses a quantitative method to ascertain and consider the influence of each contact by its ability to build attitudes towards brands in the category. Based on statistical modelling, it is both a planning and evaluation tool, concentrating on how particular kinds of marketing communications (or competitor activity and press coverage) change brand perceptions.

There are three key stages in Cognitive Tracking:

1. Consumers in specific audience or market segments talk about the brand in their own words – generating perhaps 20 key 'brand associations' that define and differentiate that brand. This work is done in qualitative research.

2. Hard data is gathered from survey research – allowing brand associations to be quantified alongside a bank of data about exposure to marketing communications activity. ('Exposure' is based on recognition of actual marketing communications material – perhaps hundreds of pieces of stimulus material are necessary in each 6-monthly wave).

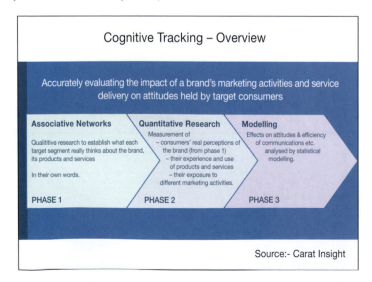

3. Statistical modelling identifies how brand perceptions have changed as a result of communications exposure. The methodology allows cause & effect to be demonstrated, and is robust enough to provide a rigorous assessment of many channels – without relying on consumers to attribute influence to particular comms channels, as traditional tracking (and some newer approaches) would.

Cognitive Tracking has been used to support the communications channel planning for Guinness and other major clients. In the example below, for retail bank Abbey, the system highlighted how the perceptions of three different consumer segments were being driven by different combinations of activity (e.g. communications, press coverage, service experience).

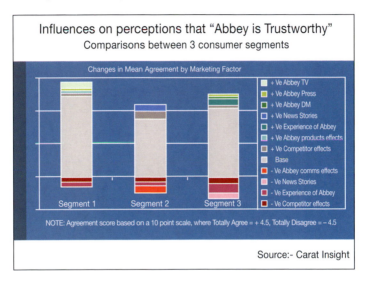

Finally, another model, known as Second Sight, has recently completed its pilot stage at media planning and buying agency Universal McCann. It is again single-source, and again multichannel, and also focuses on outcomes (such as purchasing) rather than just proxy measures (such as OTS or brand awareness).

Second Sight, Universal McCann

Aims:
- for communications planners: data source that identifies the relationship between communications exposure, brand awareness, brand equity and purchasing behaviour, in the form of a desktop system they can interrogate and manipulate.

- for clients: a way to understand the effect of various communications activities on the sales performance of their own and competitor brands; obtain guidance on issues including brand switching, loyalty, trial, portfolio management, customer acquisition, etc.

Approach:
- ongoing consumer panel of 3000 respondents.

- initial benchmark survey of whole sample covering brand awareness, brand attitudes and brand purchase behaviour, plus a diary-based assessment of their media consumption in a 'typical week'.

- on a 3-month rotation, matched sub-samples participate in a detailed media diary (per half-hour) detailing all communications they are consuming – as well as a repeat of the brand health questionnaire.

- communications consumption week-by-week is modelled from the combination of benchmark data, diary-week data, and existing industry media surveys.

- analysis incorporates detailed knowledge of client (and some competitor) communications activity: sourced from industry data on above-the-line media, and direct from client on promotions, sponsorships, direct mail and door drops, etc.

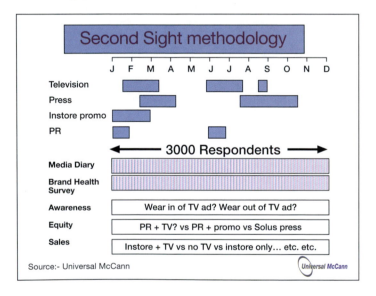

As the chart shows, the system can assess the purchasing behaviour of each individual before, during and after the advertising/promotion, and learn about their exposure to advertising or promotions.

An example of where this has been applied to a client problem is for Nescafé Gold Blend. The methodology allows for a more rigorous assessment (than a simple tracking study) of which combination of channels was the most effective at shifting brand attitudes:

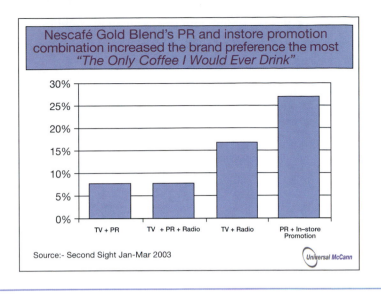

Nescafé Gold Blend's PR and instore promotion combination increased the brand preference the most
"The Only Coffee I Would Ever Drink"

Source:- Second Sight Jan-Mar 2003

Universal McCann

The potency of all of these approaches lies in the potential to make like-for-like comparisons between channels competing for role and budget in the communications mix. These are pioneering approaches, mirrored by innovative work being done by major brand owners, and all have the potential to become powerful evaluation and planning tools.

Some final thoughts

The intention in this chapter has been to set out the challenges and the opportunities for doing a good job of evaluation. Ultimately this offers the seductive long-term prospect of real progress in objectivity (all the options have been properly considered) *and* effectiveness (the best strategy pursued, with proof it was best). But, given consumers' current relationship with brands and organisations, the fast-changing media-entertainment landscape, and the emergence of new platforms for marketing, such confidence and predictability remains as elusive as ever. A desire to conduct careful and intelligent evaluation will draw attention to key issues in media neutral planning, like being clear about roles to be played by channels and being specific about objective-setting for the channels performing those roles.

A real fear is that the desire to pin down the last penny will detract from big-picture thinking, concentrating on media-spend economies at the expense of broader content quality and delivery. A too-obsessive attention to accountability leads to marketing that is risk-averse and closes the door to new opportunities. Disciplined evaluation should provide the necessary support structure for creativity and leap-making marketing thinking, and as most marketers dearly wish, decision making with the CEO on board. For this reason, evaluation should never be only about the numbers, but about instinct, hence our inclusion of qualitative techniques, as well as the powerful tools of tracking and econometrics.

At the beginning of this section we said that evaluation could be both an obstacle and a gateway to the achievement of media neutral planning. We have provided evidence of a willingness to adapt existing methods, and of the courage to develop new ones. It means that evaluation approaches are indeed emerging to respond to the challenge of media neutral planning and to advance the quality of communications decision-making and the impact of marketing activity on business performance.

Notes and References

(1) The Interactive and Direct Marketing Guide, IDM

(2) www.ipr.org.uk

Afterword

... comments welcome ...

This book sets out to describe how leading marketing companies and communication agencies are dealing with the task of media neutral channel choice in an environment where the scope and nature of the channels themselves are changing all the time. Whether we have recorded 'best' practice is no doubt a moot point but we are confident that we have found some good and sensible practice. Top of the list may be Diageo and Unilever, both of whom have straightforward logical approaches which implicitly demonstrate the importance of a constant investment in comprehensive consumer information. We have also encountered a number of models, some of which seem to approach channel planning in ways which are potentially exciting. But the task cannot be dealt with by a single procedure; the roots of channel planning lie right back in the brand positioning and marketing objectives. Indeed, media neutral planning can be regarded as the whole marketing problem seen from a channel choice standpoint.

Media neutral planning is a continuum from objectives to final execution which, by and large, is being shouldered by client companies themselves. Attempts to get agencies of different specialisms to work together have frequently foundered because of turf wars about roles and budgets, but they have also come unstuck because relatively few agency-side people have a sufficient range of skills and knowledge to approach the job with confidence – which is something agency managements may need to ponder.

We hope that this book has captured a sufficiently broad spectrum of thinking and ideas to be useful to people reading it. That said, we recognise that the communications industry is diverse and ever-changing. Almost at the moment of printing the book goes out of date. So perhaps success is when we get a response like 'you've left us out' and 'here is an important theme you have not paid enough attention to'.

If that's how you feel, please do get in touch. Our email addresses, and short biographies, can be found on pages 146 & 147.

Don Cowley *(Managing Editor)* is a partner in Langham Works. This agency has been set up to provide a community of marketing communication skills, including channel neutral planning. He has edited two previous books for The Account Planning Group – *How to plan advertising* and *Understanding Brands*.

don.cowley@langhamworks.co.uk

Julian Saunders *(Editor)* is co-founder of The Joined Up Company, which advises blue chip clients on communications strategy. He has previously been planning director at Ogilvy, Executive Planning Director at McCann-Erickson and Chief Executive at red cell advertising.

julians@joinedupcompany.com

Roderick White has spent years in ad agencies as planner and consultant, in the UK and internationally, covering a vast range of categories. As a writer on marketing communications, he now edits *Admap*. His books include leading textbook *Advertising* (McGraw-Hill).

Roderick_White@warc.com

Janet Grimes formed her own company in 2002 eponymously titled "Janet Grimes Strategy & Planning". She is a communications strategist and planner with broad experience in many communications channels having worked in publishing, PR, advertising (for 20 years) and the digital field.

jgrimes@btinternet.com

Peter Crawshaw held senior marketing roles with Reuters and Bertelsmann before setting up his own communications consultancy *integratedcommunication*. He has worked with a wide range of media including PR, DM and Digital, and has experienced first hand the challenges of delivering effective multi media campaigns and media neutral planning.

peter@integratedcommunication.co.uk

Tony Regan was a pioneer of 'media strategy' at HHCL, then a founding partner of Michaelides and Bednash, recently described as 'the high priests of media neutral planning'. Since then he has been Joint Managing Director at media agency PHD and now runs his own consultancy, Brand Performance.

Tony@brandperformance.com

Marie-Louise Neill is Strategic Development Director at Research International and current APG Chair. She has over 15 years planning experience, culminating in the multi-channel communications plan for the launch of the euro, the largest public information campaign ever conducted.

M.Neill@research-int.com

Acknowledgements

Editorial Acknowledgements
We would like to thank the following organisations for their help and encouragement.

IPA	ISBA
DMA	IAB
IPR	IDM
Media Circle	Centre for integrated marketing
Royal Mail	

Chapter One
Melanie Howard, Yasmine Baladi – Future Foundation
Julian Bond – Research International
Mindshare
Adam Morgan – Eat Big Fish
Robert Heath – Value Creation
Simon Litton, Danny Meadows-Klue – Interactive Advertising Bureau
Andrew Harrison – Nestlé UK
NOP

Chapter Two
Michael Harvey – Diageo
Craik Jones
Alan Rutherford – Unilever
Sheila Byfield – Mindshare
Mary Stewart-Hunter – OMD Europe
Carat
MicroMatch
Admap
Alfa Romeo GB
MediaCom
Mars Ltd
Siamack Salari – Everyday Lives
Claydon Heeley
Clare Rossi – WWAV
WARC.com
David Smith – Citygate DVL Smith

Chapter Three
Marco Rimini, Convenor of Judges – IPA Effectiveness Committee, 2002
Angus Jenkinson, Professor of Integrated Marketing – University of Luton
Seb Royce, Creative Director – Glue

MT Rainey – RKY&R
Rory Sutherland, Creative Director – Ogilvy One
Kim Papworth, Creative Director – Wieden & Kennedy
Stuart Archibald – Archibald Ingall Stretton – and Fallon, for Skoda
Richard Warren – Delaney Lund Knox Warren for Halifax
Jo Reid – Lowe Partners Worldwide for Stella Artois
Neil Dawson – TBWA
Ailana Kamelmacher and Tony Regan for innocent
Dan Izbicki – WCRS for Orange
Russell Davies – Wieden & Kennedy for Honda
Ashley Alsup – BBH for Johnnie Walker
Bill Scott & Gwen Raillard – BBH for Lynx
Tania Forester – Lowe Partners Worldwide
The Marketing Store for Larazade
Alan Wilson & Tina Kaye (Planning Consultant)
Adrian Zambardino – Saatchi & Saatchi
Mark Fiddes – Euro RSCG Partners

Chapter Four
Angus Jenkinson, Professor of Integrated Marketing – University of Luton
NINAH Consulting, part of Zenith Optimedia Group
Alan Branthwaite – CRAM International
Jonathan Durden, Chairman – PHD
Whiskas – Mars Petfood
Jon Wilkins – Naked
Karen Gregory, Senior Marketing Manager – COI, Dept Health
Ian Priest – VCCP
Will Lever – mmO$_2$
Michael Harvey – Diageo
Bruno Rost, Corporate Press Relations – Experian
Martin Miller
Consumer Division Marketing – BT
Jeff Hyams – Zed, Zenith Optimedia
Fiona Blades – Claydon Heeley Jones Mason
Jeff Taylor – One-One
Andrew Goulborn Rise Communications – Integration-MCA©
Yellow Pages
Frank Harrison – Zenith Optimedia-Media DNA
Iain Jacob – Starcomm Motive
Philip Rumbol, Marketing Director – Stella Artois
David Kyffin – Media Com Direct
Nick Cross – Egg
Dilys Maltby, Partner – Circus

Acknowledgements (continued)

Liz Cook, Marketing Communications Manager – Floodline
Jeremy Taylor – Langham Works
Stephen Gray – Chrysler Jeep UK
David Moynihan – WCRS for MINI

Chapter Five
Marie Oldham – Media Planning Group
Fiona Greggains
Proximity
Matthew Higgins – First Direct
Sally Dickerson – MGOMD
Billet Consultancy
Claire Spencer – i to i tracker
Terry Prue – HPI
Geoff Allen – Researchcraft
Alan Wilson – Mindshare
Andrew Goulborn – Rise Communications
Kate Rowlinson – Carat
Chris Sutcliffe
Universal McCann
Jason Brownlee – Emap
Simon Foster – PHD Confidential

Production
Editorial Services – WritersServices.com
Design Consultant – Rob Oldfield Design Associates, York
Design & Typesetting – gavin ward design associates, York
Printing – Philtone Litho Ltd, Bristol

Index of Case Studies

THE COMMUNICATIONS CHALLENGE

Index

THE COMMUNICATIONS CHALLENGE